THE

LUTHERAN

WAY OF LIFE

by
Ralph W. Loew

Prentice-Hall, Inc. Englewood Cliffs, N. J.

To the men and women of the parish
whose renewing and reforming faith
is rethinking the mission of the
Church.
For such as these, I give thanks
upon every remembrance.

Library of Congress Catalog Card Number: 66-24980

Printed in the United States of America
T 54129

Prentice-Hall International, Inc., London
Prentice-Hall of Australia, Pty. Ltd., Sydney
Prentice-Hall of Canada, Ltd., Toronto
Prentice-Hall of India Private Ltd., New Delhi
Prentice-Hall of Japan, Inc., Tokyo

Contents

Preface

A Personal Introduction
to the Lutheran Way of Life

The high-vaulting lancets of the chancel windows in Holy Trinity Lutheran Church, Buffalo, are a focus of color and light. They are more. They illustrate the message and mission of the church. Here are the symbols of the Trinity, the Word and the Sacraments. The Word is the living word of God, known through the centuries through Scripture, spoken through the shared word. The God of creation is still being known through the vocation of men. The Christ is the Lord known in Incarnation and Atonement. God, speaking through apostles, martyrs, prophets, contemporary leaders is the Holy Spirit calling, enlightening, sanctifying now. The Sacraments are the evidence of our becoming what we really have been, members of the family. Symbols these.

I turn and look down the long nave, through the open windows beyond, to the rushing traffic of downtown Main Street. That's another symbol. All of this Christian message must be interpreted and translated into the life and thought-forms of the people who come in and to those who rush by. As a Lutheran, I am grateful for the heritage of freedom, for the catholicity of an historic message and for the experience of the real presence through Word and Sacrament. As a Lutheran I am also aware that it is not enough to praise the heritage; it is only understood as it is shared with those

4

on the highway, interpreted and discussed in the councils
of this age and experienced in the whole of life. It is known
through the clear glass as effectively as through the stained
glass.

To write about the Reformation, especially as a contemporary experience, is to understand Maeterlincks's tale of an
inn in Belgium. Over the doorway there were inscribed the
words, "Within me there is more." These chapters can only
indicate that there is much more within than is here expressed.

There is much more space given to the experience of
being a member of the Christian community as a Lutheran
than to historical data or precise theological statement.
This series of books on various facets of the "Way of Life"
become a dialogue of personal witness, helping the family
of believers as well as the wondering doubters to hear some
of the notes of emphasis.

At this time Lutherans around the world are preparing
for the 450th anniversary of the Protestant Reformation.
That was a time of upheaval, an age of storm and stress,
when everything "nailed down seemed to come unloosed."
Despite or because of that upsetting fragmentation, the
living Word of God is unforgettably known. Much that is
alive in our own time stems to those days.

I think of this as a parish pastor having the privilege of
living with the men and women of the congregation and
sharing with the residents of the city. We have studied the
catechism together. We have shared Scriptures together.
We have listened to some of the distinguished churchmen
and theologians together. We have tackled some of the
tough problems of our city together. I know the joy, the
frustrations and the predicaments of parish life. Yet in this
Lutheran parish I find not only the vigor and uncomplaining
willingness to study, to worship and to pray, but also a
freedom to experiment. Obviously we need theologians

to bring us fresh insights. We need brilliant administrative leaders to set the climate. But we need these men and women of the parish who quietly, significantly, and most often in ways far more impressive than they understand, become Christs one to another.

A newspaperman in Vermont received a famed recognition a few years ago because he wrote of local events from a worldwide point of view. I remember Franklin Clark Fry addressing a question to an audience in Ohio, years ago when I was at the beginning of my ministry, asking "From God's point of view, what's foreign?" The parish can become the local focus of this universal concern, knowing that nothing is foreign. I've traveled the mission fields, participated in international assemblies, seeing the facets of this Christian witness from many points of view. You can see leaders and members of the churches, shaken by wars, troubled by the political pressures, disturbed by the indifference of secularism, living through extraordinary circumstances with extraordinary commitment. I know some of these leaders, missionaries and churchmen personally. They are, more clearly than these pages, the Lutheran Way of Life!

The heritage of the Reformation is a widespread complex tradition. Luther didn't spring into history without predecessors and colleagues. The whole pageantry of witness through the early centuries, the loosed spirits of Savonarola, Huss and Wycliffe, as well as the other reformers who now spoke, such as Calvin and Zwingli, are a part of the story. These pages must tell of one important strand of this Protestant witness.

Lutheranism as an organized group was born in a time of dialogue. It began as a protest, inviting discussion. Now, 450 years later, there is more encouragement for the continuation of the dialogue. To be a Lutheran is not to be an anti-Roman Catholic, or even just a pro-Protestant. Nor is it to take the heritage of the faith lightly. Certainly, it is not to live in isolation. In the same responsible freedom in which the discussion of Christian faith and life arose, it must and can be continued until we discover a new unity of the Christian household.

Introductory pages are an opportunity to thank those who have shared in the writing. I think of pastors and teachers whom I have known. I am grateful for a father who had been a member of the Lutheran Church-Missouri Synod, a mother who was an active member of a Lutheran Church in the old Joint Synod of Ohio, now the American Lutheran Church, and then through dint of circumstances for the pastor and congregation of the Lutheran Church in America. These are treasured personal contacts with the whole Lutheran family. I remember gladly the excellence of teachers and the friendship at Capital University and of Hamma School of Theology. There were also the teachers at Ohio State University, the Federated Faculty at the University of Chicago and Union Theological Seminary who stirred new yearnings.

Two men stand as symbols, representing the quality and ministry of so many others. John Olaf Evjen, Norwegian by background but catholic by scope of mind, was a Professor at Hamma School of Theology, a nonconformist scholar who shared his demanding discipline and concern for excellence with his students. He is one of many scholars and teachers who give so much to students who are emerging from their more parochial backgrounds into a new way of life.

There was Oscar Fisher Blackwelder in Washington, beloved friend and mentor, brilliant preacher, and most of all a Christian gentleman at home anywhere, with whom I had the joy of working for almost seven years. He was a living witness of the joy as well as the heartache of this way of life. He was an interpreter at its scintillating best.

Mention these two and there are hosts of others, each of them meaningful. They illustrate the essential insistence that the church must bring its best in its own original and relevant way, as it speaks to and shares in the life of today.

Virginia Beer, Florence Schlyer, Alice Niederhauser, Ruth O'Rourke and Barbara Worrall have all assisted in typing the several versions of various sections of the manuscript. The colleagues at Holy Trinity Church are a constant joy as we work together for new meanings of this way of life.

Most of all, there is Maxine, who has shared in all of these pages, who is the constant colleague and whose daily witness is the encouragement through which any of this is made possible.

The members of Holy Trinity Church, in varying ways, share in making this congregation a kind of laboratory for a Lutheran Way of Life. Whatever else these pages indicate, I pray that they witness in part to the gratitude that I feel for a heritage and an opportunity which is my personal joy, a communion in which I have lived my life and to which I owe more than I can adequately state.

I

The Growing Edge

O sacred Ardor, Comfort sweet!
Make willing hearts and ready feet
That, come what may, in storm and test
We answer only thy behest.
—*M. Luther*

Every age poses questions, and from the answers come the movements of history. In the twentieth century some of the questions are, "How can man use skills and scientific knowledge to achieve security and comfort? How can man discover the meaning of his universe? How can man defeat disease by new drugs and poverty by humanitarian measures? What is the *self?* What is the destiny of the human being? How can human beings live together? Can we preserve life on this planet?" Out of the answers to such questions come the political and social experiments as well as the philosophical, sociological and theological insights.

In the sixteenth century there was a different set of questions. How can the love of God be known and expressed? What is the liberty of the Christian? Is the Roman Church the only one through which God speaks to man? Such questions as these marked the growing edge for the development of many urgencies which coincided and focused in that dynamic movement known as the Reformation. Because of that "tragic necessity," it is concerned that the

9

same Gospel meet the questions of the twentieth century.

Lutheranism began as a protest and became a significant witness. It started as a debate; it developed as a continuing expression of the Christian Church. Today the growing witness of this confessional body gathers a diversity of cultural and social emphasis into a distinctive Christian community. A doctrinal consciousness, an evangelical loyalty, an ardent sense of freedom, a strong cultural unity and a dynamic urgency have typified this family of Christians which defies an easy jamming into a carton. The 75 million Lutherans live principally in Germany, Norway, Sweden, Denmark, Finland, Iceland, the Baltic States, Poland, Hungary, Austria, the Netherlands, Czechoslovakia, Romania, France, Australia, United States and Canada. Several million more are in the churches which are increasingly indigenous in nature in South America, Africa, India and the Far East. Among the 42 million or more refugees, who have been resettled in many places of the world since 1942, are a vast number of Lutheran families. Many of these unwilling refugees from the Baltic States and East Zone Germany, as well as from Hungary and Poland, have found new homes in countries ranging from Australia to the United States and Canada.

Such a melange of languages and local customs obviously posed problems. Sometimes it created cultural islands; at other times it provided the channel for a meaningful tradition. The contrasts of the plain worship of the Lutheran Free Church, the ornate celebration of the Mass in a Swedish Church or the great assemblage of laymen at the German Kirchentag become various reflections of a common worship. Each of them carries the notes of the resounding confessions of faith, the singing of the great chorales, and the strength of an inner unity.

These confessions of faith have sometimes been regarded as divisive or exclusive. To typify a church as "confessional" is simply to indicate that it has a theological structure and that it has attempted to state its faith concerning an understanding which has come through Scripture. This "confession" or "concordia" has been a unifying factor. As the ecumenical development of this century grows from a warming, brotherly desire to be together into structural unity, these confessions become a means to an end. They help to indicate one step on the road toward unity. The confessions are "a touchstone of truth over against every falsification and distortion of God's Word . . . The Lutheran confessions are ecumenical documents which do not self-consciously call attention to themselves; rather, in as clear and unmistakable language as possible, they call attention to Christ who is the Gospel of God." [1]

Lutherans are aware of a confessional agreement. The common acceptance of the *Augsburg Confession*, the *Book of Concord*, the *Schmalkald* and especially the *Large Catechism* and *Small Catechism* mark the core of a theological stability. These confessions, or statements of faith, are historic and unifying but not treated as infallible, binding documents. If you look for the marks of this family of Christians you find it in a doctrinal awareness, an educational emphasis, a cultural appreciation, a catholic tradition, and a compassionate concern. This heritage, preserved and enriched through the years, is now shared in the interchurch discussions of our age. Yet a church dare not canonize its traditions. The ecumenical consciousness has been inherent in these open-ended confessions. These were not, nor could have been expressed where Lutheran groups were more defensively concerned with their own cultural existence, yet the very understanding of the nature of the church drives the Lutheran into contact with his fellow-Christian. Confessions of faith are dynamic and must be expressed as an historic witness of a living faith.

As a result, concerned Christians are re-examining their

own heritage, not to instill a separatism but rather to bring the total resources of the church into an ecumenical dialogue. The Lutheran Church is not a museum but a movement. It must study and be studied. Just as it has shaped an influence, so it has been influenced by the forces which surge through this age. In some instances its stance has been cultural or ethnic rather than theological. "Our problem is, therefore, how to get in touch again with the masses of the unfaithful faithful," insists Prof. Regin Prenter of Denmark.

Luther was in constant rebellion against static forms. Bold searcher for the truth, he was in despair in his own agonizing search for peace as well as with any idolizations of the church. Lutherans around the world have known a similar suffering. They have confronted the arrogance of nationalism. They have withstood the affronts of divisions. They have fled with their scraps of clothing and their burning faith. They scattered the pages of the New Testament along the frozen wastes of the Karelian Peninsula as they fled across Finland. They suffered as lonesome theologians struggling with the meaning of the Word in prison cells as they watched their own country devastated by madness. Something was real and whole when the world seemed to be, as John Donne said, "all in pieces, all coherence gone." Something had structure but the form had meaning only because it was a living faith.

This sense of a confessional urgency in the time of national disaster is known as well in a time of ideological tension. Just as the contemporary Christian has no need to refight the battles of the sixteenth century, so he ought not to come into the present debate ignorant of his history. To do this would be a form of insanity. We are always on the edge of learning. What we believe or state as a way of life must be based on Scripture and so be relevant to our times. It must be a way of life for *now*. In these accepted confessions there is the repeated statement, "Our churches teach . . ." It is in this insistent dynamic of teaching that the statement of faith continues as an influence.

An almost forgotten illustration of this constant dialogue exists in the formulation of "The Wittenberg Articles of 1536." Bishop Fox and his colleagues in England had requested Luther to come to Britain to conduct a series of conversations looking toward some form of agreement. Deemed impractical by the Elector of Saxony who feared for Luther's life, the discussions were held by the exchange of couriers. After months of discussion, 16 articles were approved and duly signed. They represent a four-century-old precedent for the ecumenical climate of our own time. It is in such a historic consciousness, and not in the ignoring of history, that true ecumenicity arises. Lutheranism of today is challenged to mark its heritage, depict its gifts, and to bring these, with a sense of dynamic risk, into the conversations of the present.

Luther is remembered as a religious genius rather than as a systematic theologian. His break with the church of his day was not a rupture which had been carefully thought out step by step. Out of his personal agony he came to certain conclusions. At the same moment other decisions were being made in Rome which came into conflict with certain political developments in other countries. The coincidence of these movements resulted in the formation of new divisions of the Christian Church instead of the Reformation of the existing church. Luther would be dismayed to know that there are still Christians on the earth bearing his name. He would join those who yearn for the day when the basic Christian way of life may be freed from the necessity of using his name. Until that day the name of Luther will be associated with a world-wide community of believers that constitutes one important segment of the Christian Church.

The roots of the faith of this company of believers is in the total history of Christianity. Although the Christians of the sixteenth century differed in their interpretation of Christianity, there *is* a common heritage. This is of paramount importance in our conscious awareness in the twentieth century. In the current dialogue there is an attempt to find this common heritage. We share a common destiny.

In this sense there is no Lutheran Way of Life. There is a Lutheran interpretation of the Christian Way of Life. Nor can any objective observer overlook genuine differences between Lutheran groups. These differences concern the important and continuing theological dialogues which search for the strengthening of an organic as well as a spiritual unity. These differences are not just the result of personal whims or unrestrained individualism. At their best, they are the expression of a faith springing from an obedience to the Gospel. If this descriptive statement, which points to some aspects of Lutheranism, were just to become laudatory of denominationalism, it would be un-Lutheran. Any lack of self-criticism stifles the reforming principle which is the genius of dynamic Lutheranism. By its very nature this faith demands a continuing self-criticism.

Likewise there is a Lutheranism which is not limited to denominational organization. The Lutheran emphasis cannot be limited to a denomination. The name is unimportant; it is this search for and love of truth that is important, real, and contemporary.

Meanwhile, 450 years after the Reformation, Lutheranism today is a company of believers, a wave of constantly renewing faith, and it is to this group that this book is dedicated. Because there is a very definite theological structure, these Lutherans constantly debate among themselves, to the distress of many, within and outside of their ranks. Yet they stand together with a remarkable sense of community. It becomes increasingly clear in this world that while there is an opportunity to witness, this common faith must be expressed in an uncommon way. The free flow of God's Word must reach into every conceivable situation. As believers, concerned with the Christian witness which is a minority in our world, we seek for this common way. The Christian faith can be weakened by sentimentalization. It can be lost by secularization. It can be obscured by rationalism. It can be defeated by individualization. It needs actualization.

II

At the Entrance:

Worship

A mighty Fortress is our God
A trusty shield and weapon
He helps us free from every need
That hath us now o'ertaken.
　　　　　　—M. Luther

The Church might be a cathedral with its vaulting arches, or a simple frame structure in the rural heartlands. The language might be Swedish, Norwegian, Danish or German or any of the number of European or Baltic tongues. In America, the service of worship will almost always be in English.

The vestments may be stark black or a flowing white surplice with richly-embroidered stoles or perhaps an alb and chasuble. The service can be chanted or spoken. Sharing in the varying forms of worship will be a congregation of believers who witness that God was in Christ, reconciling the world unto himself. This fact of grateful adoration is the heartbeat of its existence and the lifeblood of its expression. This is the Lutheran church at worship.

Flowing through these diversities is a common theme which is ideally marked by the serene presence of God and the faith of the believer. If this seems to be no different from any number of other Christian churches at worship, this is a correct observation. There is a note of similarity and a point of contact between such worship and the

Roman Mass or the Quaker meeting. For the Lutheran at worship, there is the conscious awareness of this meeting of God and man, the dialogue between God and his family. At the heart of all worship, as simple and diversified as the variations in a Bach fugue, is the common theme, "God was in Christ, reconciling the world unto Himself." This grace and love of God invades the whole of worship and the whole of service.

The Lutheran Church, almost alone among Protestant churches, is known by the name of a man. This has been its glory and its embarrassment. The genius of Martin Luther has marked the worship and faith of the church; since he was a man of his generation, both the idolater and the debunker shared a kind of field day in trying to analyze, understand and explain this religious leader. Without entering the lists to engage in more of this battle, it is notable to understand that at the heart of Luther's faith and life was the trust that God's Word is not a remote abstraction but a revealed reality. It was God's grace, not man's. "Faith is a lively reckless confidence in the grace of God." Lutheranism expresses this emphasis most notably in its worship.

Worship reveals the closest tie with this vital dialogue in faith. "Thank God, a child seven years old knows that the church is, namely, the holy believers and the lambs that hear their Shepherd's voice. For the children pray thus, 'I believe in a holy Christian church.' Such holiness does not consist in surplices, tonsures, long clerical gowns and other ceremonies of theirs, fabricated by them without the warrant of Holy Writ, but in God's Word and in true faith." [1] An obvious oversimplification but here is the spirit of Lutheranism,—a conviction that only in the true worship of God will man respond in grateful service to God and honest service to his fellow man. To incarnate this is to have a way of life.

The Evidences of Worship • Whatever the church, in whatever language, there will be an altar and a pulpit; symbols communicating the principles of worship. The pulpit is there with its desk bearing the open Bible so that the altar might not become a fact in isolation from the Word. On most occasions the Lutheran at public worship bows for a moment of prayer in his pew and then takes in his hands a hymnal which bears the accrued experience of worship of the Christian centuries. Here are the liturgical orders, the ancient collects from all ages of Christendom and the suggestions for worship which have become customary for the Christian. Most of them bear, in very small print, the suggestion, "Here the Pastor may." It is this flexible freedom which typifies this form of worship. All things are possible within the church, when properly understood; nothing should be permitted as an entity. "God's Word cannot be without God's people; on the other hand, God's people cannot be without God's Word." [2] Here is the discipline of orderliness and the freedom of creative worship. Whatever the difference in some matters, the form of worship is a unifying factor, for almost all Lutherans in America use the same book of worship. Within a few years, a common service book and hymnal will be compiled for national usage.

The Fact of Worship • The rejection of everything that is an obstacle to man's understanding of God's Word and the acceptance of things which permit this understanding, have marked this form of worship at its best. Thus holy water, rosaries, or other physical symbols (adiaphora) could be rejected; when rightly understood, they might be kept. It is the preaching and teaching of the Word that is central and if there is a rite or act which does not permit this understanding of God's Word, then that ceremony can and must be rejected, or at least interpreted in its proper sense. The Christian confronts God in a tension of fear and gratitude, in trembling and confidence, reflected in his private and corporate worship.

Worship is not an act which encourages rewards in the sense that a man might wish a halo because he attended church services. One does not please God in this way. Worship is the free response of man's faith to God's promise. To accept, understand and express this promise is the way of faith. This he will express in a multitude of ways for it is basic to his sense of vocation, the experience and the understanding of his hopes. God and man! Not the church! Or ethics! Or the State! Always God, through Christ, reconciling man unto himself!

There are two kinds of believing: first a believing about God which means that I believe that what is said of God is true. This faith is rather a form of knowledge than a faith . . . Men possessing it can say, repeating what others have said, I believe that there is a God. I believe that Christ was born, died, rose again for me. But what real faith is, and how powerful a thing it is, of this they know nothing.

There is, secondly, a believing in God, which means that I put my trust in Him, give myself up to thinking that I can have dealings with Him and believe without any doubt that he will be and do to me according to the things said to Him. Such faith which throws itself upon God, whether in life or death, alone makes a Christian man.[3]

Because of this awareness, there is the statement of the faith of the Church as a part of its worship. *The Apostles' Creed* or the *Nicene Creed*, the two most frequently used statements, are not boxes into which one crams believers, but platforms upon which the believers stand. They offer a common footing. The congregation is at this moment expressing in its own recognizable diversities the free flow of faith in this world. These creeds are statements of faith gathering the whole family of Christians into a community of believers. These creeds enable the community as well as the individual to say "I believe." [4]

The Lutheran confession of faith and of sin can be stated in today's world through these uniting expressions of faith. The confessional aspects of worship bring men to the knowledge of God's righteousness and mercy. They will differ in their interpretations as a child and a Doctor of Philosophy differ in their understanding of the words, "I believe that God has created me and all that exists." Each sees truth and perhaps the child sees more than the learned man. Each sees by God's grace, and neither need feel that the ancient confession is a binding limitation. We will have to work together for we have prayed for one another and worshipped the God and Father of all.

To stand in a Lutheran congregation and recite the words of the Creed is to become linked with the heritage of the past and the communion of the present. We are not singly a collection of individuals, an aggregate audience with a dissimilar togetherness. The prayers and the creeds of the church become the expression of the universal need of forgiveness and the common understanding that there is a truth beyond our truth, and a forgiveness beyond our own amends. So Luther vigorously writes:

And this is the reason that our doctrine is most sure and certain, because it carries us out of ourselves, that we should not lean to our own strength, our own conscience, our own feeling, our own person, and our own works; but to that which is without us, that is to say the promise and the truth of God which cannot deceive us.[5]

The Essential Form of Worship · Worship is never limited to the formal liturgy nor dimensioned within the church. The Word cannot be confined to a pulpit and altar. This is one focus of worship but it is not the complete dimension. Lutherans may not always sense this, and Dietrich Bonhoeffer scathingly attacked a distortion of God's grace as "cheap grace." The whole of life is involved. To make a formal service the sole form of worship is to indulge in a kind of idolatry. To rule it out or neglect it is to reject an important form of clothing of God's word. This tension is evident where there seems to be little concern for public worship. In these same situations there could be a general discussion of the principles of Christian faith and life as taught in the schools and debated in its forms of culture. Thus, the American may worship more regularly and discuss his faith less knowledgeably than some of his European counterparts, who might reverse this process. There is no division between grace and discipleship, between worship and service.

At its heart and true best, worship is the recapturing of the traditional heritage of Christian experience. It is not something which started in the sixteenth century. It is rather the translation of the forms of the centuries into the language of the people that the free expression of God's Word may be known and understood. Any division here is non-Lutheran. For Luther, the Word was God's revealing act whether in sermon, prayer or hymn. To pull these apart or to make any of them superior acts of obeisance are equally wrong. Worship is a uniting act in the believer that fulfills God's living Word through words, acts and deeds.

In its earliest existence these worship forms were the translation of the Mass. The later statements of worship still owe their origins to a dynamic growth in the centuries of Christian experience, not to something which has been decided upon by the individual pastor and congregation. In brief, the agenda contains:

The Invocation in the Name of the Trinity
The Confession of sins (We are by nature sinful and unclean . . .)
The Declaration of God's absolving Grace (Kyrie Eleison, the Gloria in Excelsis, the Salutation and Collect)
The Reading of the Word of God (Epistle and Gospel)
The Statement of Faith (Apostles' or Nicene Creed)

The Word of God in the Life of Believer (The Sermon and
Sacraments)
The Response to the Good News (Offering)
The Prayer of the Church (Pastoral prayer or General Prayer of
Praise and Intercession)
The Benediction

In general this form of service is known and understood
in all of the churches called "Lutheran." By Confessions,
the Lutheran is free from liturgical rigidity; in practice a
recognized form based on tradition and experience is followed. This is the clothing of the Word, and its only demanding requirement is that in every form the truth and
grace of God shall be known and communicated.

The Focus of Worship • If the forms seemed to represent
diversity in their capturing of ancient liturgical practices
(the Lutheran hymnody carries the Latin and Greek terms
such as *Gloria in Excelsis* or *Kyrie Eleison*), they also express the faith that Christ is a living Presence binding this
diversity in unity. The Cross or Crucifix on the altar is a
focus, an understood but not essential symbol of God's
coming to man. The pastor may or may not turn to the
altar when he prays or speaks or chants the liturgy in
antiphonal responses with the congregation, as the symbol
of the dialogue between God's presence and man's faith.
The pastor and the congregation are held by their faith in
God's atoning act and forgiving grace which this cross
now represents.

When the Scriptures are read, the congregation usually
stands at the statement of the Gospel but remains seated
for the reading of the Old Testament or the Epistles of
the New Testament. The worshipper stands as he would
if the President entered, and he sits as he would when he
eagerly reads a letter from home. Again, this is the reverent
symbol of the living presence of Christ expressed in a
visual or dramatic form. The focus of worship is neither

altar nor liturgy but the ever-present witness of Christ. Faith is hearing the Word and partaking of the Sacraments and discovering this living presence of Christ. To isolate worship from the daily deeds of man is to miss the impact of the Good News. In the hearing of the Gospel and in the shared act of the Sacrament the congregation and the pastor participate in a communal experience. It is only in the experience (the acceptance of the presence of Christ) that there is validity in worship. So Christ, not just his words or the statements of his acts, becomes the heart of worship.

The prayers may be ancient in setting or free in the vocabulary of the present. The hymn may be an ancient chorale or in a modern setting. The liturgy may be richly embossed with the traditional expression. Yet there will be orderliness, reverence, and the recognition of this presence of Christ. It will be a Christian worship which is not limited to organization or to form, yet not separated from either. As the church is a people of God, so in the forms of worship the communion of saints understands God and faith.

The Language of Worship · Unwittingly, man is likely to associate God's word with his native language and cultural heritage. This has been a parochial problem of Lutheran churches through the years. The coming of great waves of immigrants to the United States enabled these ardent Christians to bring their expression of this living Word in the garb of individual language. This was to be expected. When they wanted to limit this worship to this language and cultural forms, they were in trouble.

There is the pious German who insisted that "German was the language in which to worship; English the language with which to make money" who caricatured this dilemma. Because churches insisted on limiting worship to a language or a cultural pattern, they fell into word-traps violating their own principles. The Lutheran faith insists upon the free flow of Word to all people, in each man's language and in all natural expressions which incarnate this living Word. Luther himself devoted some of the major efforts of his career to translating Scripture into the language of the people. In his "Essay on Translation" he tells of going into the market place and "looking into the mouths of the people" before he put the translation of the Scriptures into words.[6] It is this coming into the coinage and commerce of conversation which typified the Lutheran way of life. Whenever there is a neglect of communication, this lack becomes its barrier.

This burden of culture has preserved colorful values. It has kept alive the heritage of peoples. It provided an environment of security during the difficult years of adaptation to a new country. It became a barrier when it confronted the need of witnessing to others who thought of these people as alien. Today this is ancient history in the Lutheran Church. In the American church there is the residue of a great tradition in worship, nowhere typified with greater dignity and lucid sharing of a world-wide experience than in *The Service Book and Hymnal*. Gathered together in one book are two complete musical settings for the worship of the church, services for Matins and Vespers, the Collects and Prayers, the Rubrics for special orders in the life of the worshipper as in baptism, confirmation, marriage and death. The Hymnal contains chorales from Germany and the Scandinavian countries as well as the melodic statements of the Christian faith which have come from every area and era of Christian experience. The service book and hymnal provides the unifying language for the community of believers.

A Singing Church · The mark of the Reformation was heard most dramatically in the involvement of the con-

gregation in worship. No longer was the priest isolated at
the altar. Now pastor and people shared in antiphonal responses, sang hymns and participated in a common worship. The liturgical renewal of the twentieth century had
its forerunner in the sixteenth. Today it seems incredible
that the use of the vernacular should have been a daring
and risky business causing consternation among Christians.
The Lutheran's sensitivity to the needs of the individual,
his insistence on continuity and his ability to blend these
two in a practical translation of the eternal into the contemporary justified any risks which he took. Music and
Word were merged into a vigorous expression of worship.
A characteristic of Lutheran worship has been the congregational singing of hymns and sharing in worship. The
vigor with which advocates of civil rights have sung "We
Shall Overcome" was the robust quality of congregational
hymn singing. The Lutheran singing A Mighty Fortress;
Lord, Keep Us Steadfast; From Heaven Above, or Now
Thank We All Our God experienced this same unifying
verve. Bach, Paul Gerhardt and a thousand others enriched
this worship which becomes a major contribution to contemporary understanding of Christian worship.[7]

The Thrust of Worship • The modern age of wars and
threats of wars has dramatically brought this meaning of
worship into focus. There were Norwegian Lutherans who
had not gone to church regularly who suddenly discovered
that in the singing of "A Mighty Fortress Is Our God"
they could defy the demonic Nazis at Trondheim. There
were Estonians who could withstand the on-rush of Com-
munists as they considered their faith. In these moments
of danger, in the concentration camps with the refugees,
in the prison houses with a Martin Niemoller, a Dietrich
Bonhoeffer or a Hans Lilje and hundreds of nameless
martyrs, or in the witness of the Gospel among the Arab

refugees in Palestine, the Lutheran has realized the essential unity of this witness of worship.

If this thrust is known in its standing against certain idolatries and cruelties, it must be known also as it expresses the free flow of the Word of God in society. The same Gospel that stands *against* a Hitler needs to stand *for* the love of God flowing to a man who is bent upon exploring space. The same faith which defied Aryan arrogance must speak daringly into the racial situation. It is to the credit of the Lutheran State Churches of Europe that they have not forbidden the free worship of other Christian groups. To believe in a gracious God is to discover that grace beyond the fence or wall erected by governments or institutions. If Lutherans have sometimes distorted this truth, the truth is still essential. To have entered into a Lutheran Church to worship is to have come into a fellowship of believers and a company of sin-conscious individuals who have found the grace of God expressed in hymns, in catechism, in the Bible, in historic liturgical forms in their own language and always in the knowledge of God's love alive among men.

The Reformation restored the sermon to an effective place in public worship and it is the sermon which still has a valid emphasis. This preaching, based on Scripture, guided by pericopal or an ancient order of textual readings but not limited or dimensioned, has been significant. The sermon is the evidence of the relevance of the Word to the world in which men live. At its best it is a living word for living people in living situations, a true channel of grace. The sermon is God's use of the gifts or experience of man; the whole of life is a more eloquent sermon.

So, as Bishop Hans Lilje has written:

The church of tomorrow, in all her branches, will resemble the church of the first centuries more than the church of the liberal era ever could. The Lutheran Church has least reason to fear these changes, for she has never attached undue importance to institutional or organizational structure. She will take her Bible, the Word of God into the coming era, she will sing her hymns in the new age. The Commandments, the Lord's Prayer, the confessions of faith will be the same amidst the changing conditions of life.

The new experiences she will need—the firmer faith in a world beyond, the readiness to sacrifice and to suffer, a more fervent charity—will not come as results of better human planning. They will come as divine gifts from God's hands, in answer to the Church's prayers.[8]

At the heart of man's pilgrimage is his worship of God and his recognition of the free responsibility of his faith. It is in this freedom that he now stands, caught in the tension of a magnificent liberty and the dread to accept this faith as a personal rather than an institutional responsibility.

The individual worshipper and his fellow-members and neighbors stand together, kneel together, worship together. Here is said the Creed with its ties to history and its stabilizing platform for today. Here is prayed the Lord's Prayer. Here are sung the hymns and the shared dialogue of worship. Here the Word is read and stated in sermon and through Scripture. Here, as in centuries past, these men, women and children pray:

For the peace that is from above and for the salvation of our souls, let us pray to the Lord:
For the peace of the whole world, for the well-being of the churches of God, and for the unity of all, let us pray to the Lord:
For this holy house and for them that in faith, piety and fear of God offer here their worship and praise, let us pray to the Lord:
Help, save, pity and defend us, O God, by thy grace:
Lord, have mercy upon us.
Christ have mercy upon us.
Lord, have mercy upon us.

The awesome worship of God, the corporate act of the church, or the private and personal devotion of the worshipper indicate the beginning, not the end. To know this

God is to send a man into alert tension with his environment and with himself. He is free to worship. Now he must be free to express this worship in his daily life. As the Christian worships, he is at the *entrance*.

Cheap grace is the preaching of forgiveness without requiring repentance, Baptism without church discipline, Communion without confession, absolution without personal confession. Cheap grace is grace without discipleship, grace without the cross, grace without Jesus Christ, living and incarnate.

"Costly grace is the gospel which must be sought again and again, the gift which must be asked for, the door at which a man must knock." [9]

The Liturgical Year • The calendar of the church year provides a remembrance of the events of the life of Christ. This suggestion of Scripture readings (pericopes) provides an orderly indication of the mighty acts of God. The sermons of the various Sundays need not be based upon these sections from the Old and New Testaments. Yet the statements are there and, almost always, used as a part of the liturgical worship of the congregation. If they are read, with the excitement of Scripture, they put the contemporary worshipper in continuing remembrance of the events in the life of Christ and of the living Church.

Hymns, liturgical responses, vestments, prayers, introits, collects and graduals all combine to provide the setting for the renewal of this experience of the Christian witness. This is the balanced rhythm which keeps the corporate worship and the personal devotion in meaningful orbit.

ADVENT, beginning four weeks before Christmas and recounting the preparation for the coming of Christ. In a time when Christmas is often banal and secularized, these are the days of a deepening experience, telling of the ministry of John the Baptist and of a world that needs to be ready to understand the coming of Christ. The color is purple, suggesting the royalty associated with Christ.

CHRISTMAS, the traditional festival, universal in its appeal and so meaningful that all too often the joy of these days escapes the real meaning of Christ's birth. For the company of believers it is the remembrance of "God among us." As John said centuries ago, the light was among us and the darkness could not put it out. That's the joy of Christmas. The color is white.

EPIPHANY, the celebration of the coming of certain men of the East. More important for today, it is the understanding that the Christian Gospel was not meant for one race or one nationality or one people. Here is the missionary thrust of the church, the insistent witness to the parochial-minded that they cannot contain this living Christ in any culture or group. The color is white.

LENT, the season of approximately forty days before Easter. It is introduced by three Sundays which still bear the old Latin terms of Septuagesima, Sexagesima and Quinquagesima. In these days of liturgical reform someone might find more meaningful statements concerning these "gesima" Sundays, based on ideas instead of numbers. Lent itself is a season of devotion, arising from the forty days Jesus spent in the wilderness. Traditionally it was a time of sacrifice and obligation. There have been those in recent times who have suggested that the season be shortened into a kind of "instant Lent" of one or two weeks. For most Lutheran churches it is still a time to suggest new ways for Christian expression and new understanding of the haunting witness of Christ. Services of worship are held in midweek. In many inner-city urban churches there are noonday services for nearby residents and workers, and there is a renewed expression of devotion.

The season closes with the climactic Holy Week, beginning with Palm Sunday and continuing throughout Good Friday. The color is purple.

EASTER, the joyous festival of the church year. The word is derived from pagan origins but the idea springs right out of the tomb. It is the time of life and the season of hope. It is the assertion that God is not contained in tombs nor defeated by men's acts or minds. The resurrection of Christ was central in the life of the New Testament church; it is central in the thinking of the renewing life of the Christian. We are in the company of the living God who is always upsetting our deadly tombs. The color is white.

PENTECOST or WHITSUNDAY, the season of God's continuing witness. Before Easter the world had seemed to come to an end for the disciples; after Easter there was a new world in which to live. Approximately forty days after Easter the disciples gathered at the celebration of Pentecost. They began to speak in languages surprising to them and understandable to others.

Recalling this event, Pentecost is regarded as a birthday of the Christian Church. The available, communicating God of power and life is known in and through the living Church.

This Sunday becomes the occasion for Confirmation of children in many congregations. The color is red.

TRINITY, beginning on the first Sunday after Pentecost, continues until Advent. How shall men speak of God? The creeds speak of Father, Son and Holy Spirit.

The catechism speaks of Creator, Saviour, Sanctifier. The Christian knows that God is before all things, in all things and beyond all things. To speak of the Trinity is to express the Christian's acknowledgment of God's supremacy. His closeness to us and the wonder of His greatness above all things outleaps our words and concepts—these are celebrated in the word "Trinity." The color is green.

FESTIVALS and SAINTS' DAYS are marked in the rubrics of the church, remembering the fact that "we are surrounded by so great a company of witnesses." The grateful remembrance of witnesses and ambassadors is the reminder of a treasure and the renewal of faith in the current crisis. These days may seem to be little more than calendar-markings in most churches. For instance, there would be few congregations keeping the Feast of St. Matthias February 24th. Yet the indication in the calendar is a reminder of the selection of the man who took the place of Judas. Once more the ranks were closed.

The Orderly Communication • The statement of suggestions for the church calendar is simply an assistant in communication. There is a flexibility in all of these matters requiring only a concern for integrity and for the understanding of those who worship together. All of this aims to proclaim that which Luther once stated, "a holy assembly and congregation upon earth of pure saints under one head, even Christ, called together by the Holy Ghost in one faith, one mind and understanding, with manifold gifts, yet one in love, without sects or schisms."

III

The Christian Encounter:

The Grace of Our Lord

Ah, dearest Jesus, Holy Child,
Make thee a bed soft undefiled
Within my heart, that it may be
A quiet chamber kept for thee.
—*M. Luther*

"Kneel down in worship before the imprints where He has stepped. We are beggars. That is true." So wrote Luther at the very end of his career. It was as though he were placing the final stamp of experience upon the soul-struggle of his lifetime. In this encounter of the Eternal with the contemporary he found the beggardom of man and the overwhelming grace of God. He was searching neither as the traditionalist nor the iconoclast but rather for the faith of the dynamic follower of a living God. It is this eternal Yes that marks the follower of such a Luther. That vitality of faith seems to get lost in scholastic arguments and institutional rigidities. It is a contradiction to bear the name Lutheran and miss this renewal of the New Testament encounter with today.

There have been times when Protestants seemed to overlook this heritage, substituting a form of piety or a sentimental legalism for a dynamic power of faith. When faith is encased in conformity instead of being set free by the transforming spirit of the grace of God, the dynamic

of this Lutheran heritage is forgotten. Nothing can substitute for this experience, neither symbols, liturgies, nor
even confessions of faith. These indicate directions, not
dimensions.

For instance, the Lutheran knows the meaning of the
law of God in order to understand the grace of God. To
know the full meaning of the law is to know the need of
the love of God. That's an encounter! To know this is to
wrestle with it in every generation and renew it in every
crisis. Those who know the depth of sin, know better the
height of grace! The Lutheran way of life does not insist
upon a sixteenth century experience. The God who convinced Martin Luther must convince us.

Dr. Joseph Sittler underscores this, stating, "This common center and glowing core of Luther's theology . . . is
faith as an independent form of apprehension, reception
and actualization of the life of God . . . What is given
in faith is not knowledge about God but God himself,
grace, love and forgiveness." [1] To see a Lutheran church is
one thing. To enter into a Lutheran way of life is to have
caught this reality and to find a glowing core for one's own
life as well as in historic statements. God is not dead; He
is and that "is-ness" is known in the experience of forgiveness. The grace of our Lord is experienced.

Christ-centered · The knowledge-explosion of the twentieth century is only the newest emphasis of the maze
through which man tries to find his way. How shall we
know this love of God? With all kinds of rivals challenging the Christian faith and with every kind of threat assail-
ing the credal statements, what can a man believe about
this love of God? Or the fact of God? "What does it
mean to have a God, or what is God," asked Luther in his
large Catechism—and he answered his question, "God is
that to which I must look for all that is good and to which

I must flee in every need." It is at this latter emphasis of every need that modern man seeks guidance. If there is a Lutheran way of life, it is in knowing that there is a need and that God speaks into that need. "To possess something on which the heart places all its reliance," this is to know God. The 166 church groups that call themselves Lutheran are agreed at this focal point.

This enormity is known through Christ, and Christ becomes more than history. Jesus is in history, for here we find the Incarnation God made manifest to us. It is not only in what Christ says and does, but in what he is that we find him as Saviour. Here is the beginning of the Christian encounter and this dynamic experience leads man to study, to explore and to witness in personal devotional life or social service. In all of the expressions of the human spirit we always find the gracious loving God.

Sometimes Lutherans have been accused of a kind of "Christo-Unitarianism" since there has been this emphasis of Christocentricity. In a small midwestern village, the residents used to say that the difference between the Lutheran and the Presbyterian church on the next corner was that the latter church began the service with the Doxology while the former ended with it. This oversimplification was more correct than they might have guessed. The Calvinist stood before the awe of God and progressed from that vantage point. The Lutheran began with the continuing redemption of forgiving love and came in the end to praise the wonder and glory of God. His act of praise becomes the continuing vocation of the Christian man which is expressed in every facet of this exciting existence. If God seems hidden, he is revealed most certainly through Christ, and it is in man's "Now" that this faith through Christ is expressed. As Dietrich Bonhoeffer once insisted as he talked about the new forms of the church that must come, "It is not for us to prophesy that day, but the day

will come when man will be called again to utter the word
of God with such power as will change and renew the
world. It will be a new language which will horrify men,
and yet overwhelm by its power."

Sin and Grace • To know Christ is to find release from
sin, but neither to forget nor to ignore the fact of sin. Sin
is a separation from God. Luther confronted it in attempts
at pilgrimages, indulgences, and even the flogging of his
body. He tried to win or achieve grace. Modern man confronts it in his psychological exploration or in his analysis
of himself. He is in search for peace. Luther wanted to
win God's justifying grace. Modern man wants to justify
himself. Luther wanted to know how to escape from God's
condemnation. Modern man wants to climb out of some
kind of personal hole he's dug for himself. Luther drove
himself into meditation and prayer by way of these deep
and struggling yearnings. Modern man drives himself so
far and then creates an escape hatch through some activity,
pleasure or tranquilizer. Yet the struggle is there. This is
the common concern for the sin that separates.

At the very heart of the New Testament evangel is the
fact that men are always confusing the grace and love of
God with some piety. The insistence of the Corinthian
letter that even giving one's body to be burned is not
enough, is reminiscent of Jesus' chiding of the Pharisee
for his prating about spiritual achievements. Tithing, praying, attending services—all of these laudable experiences
are important only if they are the overflow and not the
end in view. Sinful man has a way of using these very acts
of piety as substitutes for the encounter with his own sin.

It is at this point that the experience of Christ brings
men to a place of transforming, not conforming. If this
doesn't seem revolutionary in the twentieth century—and
it can—it was the renewal of the spirit of faith in Luther's

day. Christ was born into this world and it was Luther who emphasized the fact that you don't find the love of God by trying to escape from the world but by coming as God's man into this world. This believing is set over against work righteousness. The very basis for all of man's ethical action springs from this understanding. It is when he sees Christ not as one historic instance, but as the entering into life itself that the follower of Christ knows that God's love is his only security, that he is enabled to live as a free man. So the proclamation of the Word (kerygma), the fellowship in the Word (koinonia) and the service because of this word (diakonia) are not separate but one. To know the love of God and to find the possibility of following Christ is to hear the Word of God and do it. In the doing of it man is not to be praised. He thanks God. So you can do anything, but if it's not done from the vantage-point of love, it's lost its best meaning.

Love That's Given · The experience, and therefore the literature, of Lutheranism is filled with the understanding of the Cross of Christ. It is not morbidity but gratitude. It is the knowledge that grace doesn't come cheaply— salvation isn't earned. "God was in Christ reconciling the world unto himself." This is at the heart of the struggle. "I delivered unto you first of all that which I also received, how that Christ died for our sins according to the Scriptures."

This is not just a pointing to the act of Christ as a notable act of devotion in a world of sin; it is the experience of that love which is basic. There is a singularity about the very holiness of God which is basic to an understanding of this love. It marches into the very heart of the struggle. When men talk of the Cross of Christ while tolerating the hatreds and prejudices of their own lives, they miss the meaning of godly love. Bonhoeffer rejected this "cheap grace," this easy talking of the love of God without understanding the Cross.

For God is a God who bears. The Son of God bore our flesh, he bore the cross, he bore our sins, thus making atonement for us. In the same way his followers are also called upon to bear, and that is precisely what it means to be a Christian. Just as Christ maintained his communion with the Father by his endurance . . . To go one's way under the sign of the Cross is not misery and desperation, but peace and refreshment for the soul, it is of the highest joy.[2]

This is pure Lutheranism.

Here is the entrance of a redeeming love into the whole of life and into the whole of history. Any attempt to compartmentalize this redemption is to miss its thrust and its meaning. When that was done in terms of the church, its clergy or its acts, it was missed, hidden from our eyes. When it is kept for certain professions, it is not comprehended. Twentieth-century man hasn't fully understood this breaking of the redemptive act of God into his self-established compartments. Just as there is racial segregation, so there is a kind of class segregation, cultural segregation, or intellectual segregation. Perhaps the "death of God" debates as well as the shattering of many of the old bourgeois dimensions can help us to restate this fallacy of placing or compartmentalizing this love of God. The deed of God in Christ, occurred in a world which had and knew the Ten Commandments. If the deed is redemptive in intention and in fact, that does not deny nor abrogate the revelation of God the Creator, but rather fulfills in the strategy of redemption what man regularly fractures in the structure of creation. Redemption does not destroy creation but realizes it.

Such love is freely given. Because of this love, the Christian is free. The gospel is not a new law. This is the responsible freedom which is Christian optimism.

The Heart of the Faith • The Cross is not only on the altar; it is at the heart of the faith. It is in the Incarnation and in the Atonement, in that single sentence that one finds the full strength of the Gospel. Church, vocation, ethics, faith—all are centered here. "Behold Christ became powerless on the cross and yet here he performed his mightiest work and vanquished sin, death, world, hell, devil and all evil."

In singing *O Sacred Head Now Wounded* one can really feel that here the very nature of God is revealed. It was in the complete human-ness of Christ, not just in his physical suffering, that the hell of abandonment was known on the Cross. Knowing this is to find the greater meaning of the love that was shared. Here at the crosspiece, is the crossroads of our faith.

To know this is to understand "For God so loved the world that he gave his only begotten Son, that whosoever believeth on Him should not perish but have everlasting life." Being a Christian is no easy, saccharine thing. The Cross is the continuing reminder that there is the paradox of utter lonesomeness and utter companionship; complete loss of self and complete finding of self; complete pain before hatred and complete peace before love. "Inherent in Luther's theology of the Cross," writes Bornkamm, "is his whole doctrine of justification, his opposition to every kind of work righteousness and every concept of merit. For by this means man desires to point to something that is visible, something he has done, which justifies the pardon of God . . . Luther's phrase 'by grace alone' is only another expression of his theology of the cross." [3] So to be a Lutheran is to know this grace, and then to act by the power of it.

Sacred and Secular • Luther came into an age of a divided church. The Reformation split the organizational structure but a split in the church already existed. It was the division between the sacred and the secular; between clergy and laity; between the holiness of a rigidized piety and the world of mankind. In his vigorous way, Luther confronted this division. The loving deed of God comes into the wholeness of life, and the old separations are revealed as false. Paul's magnificent poem of triumph in the 8th Chapter of Romans is the recognition that nothing can separate us from the love of God. Wrote Luther, "But the crazy blind world does not see this, and instead despises these callings so shamefully that it must hurt a godly heart. No, says the world, why should I be in such a low secular calling? I want to serve God and be a monk, a nun, a priest, a hermit. Such impertinence increased until the world was filled with monasteries and convents and all varieties of orders and sects so that it now crawls and swarms with spiritual people everywhere."

It would be easy to think that this division of society was taken care of by the historic act of the Reformation. It is patently as necessary to understand in our time as in any other.

As Martin Marty remarked in an address in Buffalo:

Lutheranism also shares the problems of most American religious groups. Not that many of its members seem to be able to relate the faith to all the dimensions of life. A kind of sublimal secularism is present among the faithful. Regularly, they are devout members of the church but their lives do not seem to be substantially different from those around them. The American culture religion suits many of them quite well and much of the revolutionary character of modern life is screened from view in religious institutions. Many of the congregations represent a high prejudice and a great degree of clubbiness to the outsider. The perils of mere routine in spiritual life are deadening. Lutherans sometimes act as if the fact of their having been born into or having been lucky enough to have joined the church is what saved them. But they also, so long as they listen to the authority of the preached Word, are sitting on a time-bomb which can go off, as it has gone off again and again in Christian and in Lutheran history.[4]

Faith and Belief · It is quite obvious in all of this that faith is something more than the acceptance of a number of beliefs. The Lutheran Church is a confessional church; that is, it believes that the experience of God and man has been stated in creeds and confessions of faith which are historically important and serve as foundations for the present encounter. Honoring these confessions and regarding them as inherent in the very structure of the Christian community requires more than the signing of one's name to these confessions as though they are the adoption of a treaty. To be a Lutheran is not just to sign the Augsburg Confession! Faith is the recognizing and understanding of something coming to us—or rather, Someone coming to us. The confession is the historic statement of this experience. This person-to-person relationship is recognized beyond our own search. The Confessions are symbols, recording the encounter which must be experienced in dynamic freshness again and again. The content of these statements speaks of trusting God alone—not the Confession. Faith is trusting—not another intellectual or academic activity.

To use Luther's imagery in his Christmas hymn, beliefs would become a kind of building of a cradle for the Christ; but faith is finding the very self as that cradle.

To believe this or that about God is one thing; to have faith is another. As Martin Heinecken once emphasized:

The gospel is the good news of God's coming into the right relationship of love with men in Jesus, the Christ. This revelation in Christ then also makes known that the law of all God's creation is love. Here it is revealed to the eyes of faith that behind the masks of creation stands the God of love, who has so ordered the world that community is actually possible and actively furthered. . . . Love establishes the right relationship and where this is right the whole creation is revealed as the soil and the climate in which love can flourish. But this is not an impersonal law of nature which governs things mechanically. This is a relationship between people who are free to flout the law of God and to end up in despair.[5]

So Luther defined the keeping of the first commandments as trusting in God above all things. This ultimate commitment becomes difficult for many who claim to be Christian. The man of faith isn't that man who has bundles of beliefs in his hands; he is the person, according to Luther, who is "compelled to jump from the safe shore of this life over into the abyss where we feel nothing, see nothing, and have no footing or support, but entirely at God's suggestion and with his support."

And Luther wrote, as though he were writing to our twentieth-century generation: "Faith is a living, active, mighty thing so that it is impossible for it not to do good continuously. Nor does it ask whether there are any good works to be performed; but before one can ask, faith has already performed them and is always in them . . . Faith is a living, resolute confidence in God's mercy; faith is so strong and confident that it would die a thousand times because of it." [6]

It is this understanding of man's sin and his awareness that God is involved in the whole of life that produces the encounter. God isn't locked up in churches or encumbered by the worship of the faithful. God is in the whole of life and we are meant to be in the whole of it. To encounter this love of God is to escape limiting pietisms. To encounter this love is to be a free person. That freedom is not just the escape from slavery or punishment or a degradation of man. It is the freedom for the enjoyment of life, not its abuse; for the understanding of God's presence, not an evasion. He knows that God wants him to be His own. The encounter of Christ is a constantly renewed "prodigal son" experience. We become what we are. We always were in the family, but now we know it and act like it. Basic to being a real Christian is the understanding of the grace of God that gives us this awareness. This is what we are meant to experience. It has been the shame of our churches that this has not always come through clean and clear. The fact is there, nonetheless, and it is central in all Lutheran theology. We are the witnesses of Christ-centered love in the whole of the earth. There is a theological basis for our involvement in the whole struggle. Everything is holy when it erupts from such encounter with God's love. The Lutheran Way of Life is a free response to love which is shared in a "nowness." It stands in the continuity of the holy, catholic faith and it is this renewing encounter with Christ that sends it into another confrontation with the world. It is the discovery of Christ today.

IV

The Freedom of the Christian:
Justification by Faith

> With might of ours can naught be done,
> Soon were our loss effected;
> But for us fights the Valiant One
> Whom God himself elected.
> —*M. Luther*

Justification by Faith · Ask anyone to describe the Lutheran way of life and he probably will respond with, "Justification By Faith." He may have difficulty amplifying this comment even as Lutherans have some problem in expressing this concept in twentieth-century language. Nonetheless this verse from Romans 3:28, "For we hold that man is justified apart from works of the law" is a cohesive and meaningful symbol. To know the grace of our Lord Jesus Christ is to know the possibility of justification by faith.

Christianity received a new burst of dynamic influence in the Reformation; at its heart was this understanding of grace as God's free gift and not the legalisms devised by men. For centuries men have been involved in working out the concept of freedom and the understanding of liberty. To this struggle Protestantism brings insight. It quickly reveals the sense of breaking away from the dread and fear which was a part of the religious awareness of that age. In our time the problem is not dread but nothingness; not fear of judgment but anxieties born out of meaninglessness. In Reformation days Luther talked of sin and grace; in contemporary times the Lutheran way of life is concerned with this same Gospel of hope and forgiveness that can destroy meaninglessness. To talk about justification by faith is to struggle with faith in a meaning for life, justifying man's existence now as well as in the life to come. Justification by faith alone is to be *just* before God. If this is a generation "Where man seeks out the lonely, echoing mountain walls from which he hears the agonizing mockery of his own laughter," [1] then someone must save him from a passion for Nothingness. It is here that the Gospel must be rediscovered so that man can hear another voice. That voice must be real, not just a faint echo from the past. Says Luther in the Large Catechism, "To have a god is nothing else than to trust and believe him with one's whole heart . . . If your faith and trust are right, then your God is the true God. If your trust is false and wrong, then you do not have the true God. That to which your heart clings and entrusts itself is really your God."

Emphasis · The Lutheran begins to perceive this emphasis in his study of the Catechism. Written in 1529, as a teaching technique for children, it has become a distillation of the Christian faith. A casual look at this little book reveals an immediate understanding of the gift of the Christian faith which is the foundation for freedom.

Luther understood Christ's development of the Old Testament commandments. "Ye have heard it said of old time," said Jesus, and then added, "but I say unto you." (Matthew 5:21 ff.) In each instance, the addition was the positive elaboration of the commandment and a discontent with the negative prohibitions. It wasn't enough to refrain from stealing; one had to protect one's neighbor's property. It wasn't enough to stop killing; one participates in a kind of murder with his inner hatred and his expression of unbrotherliness. It wasn't enough to condemn adultery; one could lust inwardly and build the climate for a disregard of sanctity. Thus Luther recaptures Jesus' emphasis of these positives. Understanding Christ is a key to the Old as well as the New Testament. For the Christian today, there is a lure to determine the centrality of this Christ in the search for the living God.

Grace—Not Laws • The definitions of the Commandments became miniatures of the whole landscape of Christian conduct. "We ought so to fear and to love God," he writes, "so as not to curse, swear, conjure, lie, or deceive by his name, but call upon him in every time of need and worship him with prayer, praise and thanksgiving." [2] This, instead of a mere negative condemnation of swearing.

Or, "We ought so to fear and love God so as not to slander nor to raise injurious reports against our neighbor but rather to apologize for him, speak well of him and put the most charitable construction on all his actions." What would have happened in our world if these ancient words could have been understood in the modern situation!

The *Apostles' Creed* is not an abstract statement but a personal relationship. So the fact of the Creator, God, becomes the giver of food, raiment, faculties of mind, and all the necessities of life. That stands as a reason for vocation: we ought to thank, praise, serve and obey Him. That stands as a judgment: what right does man have to waste the earth, pollute the air and poison the streams? That stands as grace: man is meant to rejoice in his use of the world.

This basis of responsible freedom becomes strikingly important in our understanding of today's problems. It is this contribution that the Christian brings to the contemporary scene. In the faith given to the Christian he finds his understanding of God's presence. In this sense he is freed from human restrictions. He is not bound to have to do things to please his neighbor, or his church or some other man-made law. He is bound to God.

Yet, out of this understanding comes his responsible freedom. He is able to be a person who is a kind of voluntary slave to his neighbor. He is truly free to serve—a "little Christ" to his neighbor. He sees Christ in his neighbor. He can do this because at the Cross, God reconciled the world unto himself. "If any man is in Christ, he is a new creature: The old things are passed away; behold all things are new." (2 Cor. 5:17)

The whole concept was boiled into one paradox which needs to be better understood in the modern world's rush into new independence. "The Christian man is the free Lord of all; therefore, the slave of no one. The Christian man is the free Lord of all; therefore, the servant of everyone." [3] This isn't doing something good in order to attain heaven or to get rewards. It is being free to serve in every possible way because he is God's man and he recognizes the reflection of this same God in his neighbor. Wherever freedom has been distorted into irreverence, liberty has become license and flexibility iconoclasm. Wherever freedom is understood "the world is charged with the glory of God." [4]

If the Christian understands that Christ's love is not a static fact but a dynamic power now, he can be delivered from a negative legalism on one hand and a kind of sterile and uncreative conformity on the other. He is free because he is bound. He is bound because he is free. At the heart of much of man's struggle in the world of politics, economics and social existence is this basic factor. His faith gives him the security—the justification—to live creatively and hopefully.

The Freedom to Expect · The concept of man as being capable of understanding that God's thrust is toward him leaves man in a tension between pessimism and optimism. He is pessimistic about man for he knows the reality of sin, the "evilness" of evil and the powers of his pride. In every age the terminology has been different but whether we speak of man's sin or his psychological perversions, it is a man's slavery to himself and his lack of freedom that is at the heart of the matter.

This sense of justification which is at the heart of Lutheranism is the understanding that one can expect God to do great things to him and through him, not necessarily *for* him. He is not going to be tempted into making religion a kind of doing of certain things or refraining from certain things in order to win God's favor. God is doing great things to him. When he understands this, he finds new perspectives for his existence. His freedom is not a rebellion but a recognition. He freely expects the greatness of God and he expects to know it.

In the world of today, man is beset by the tyrannies of other men, or the tyrannies within himself. Either he is enslaved by the restrictions of the state and the ideology of godlessness or he has his own fears. He is pressured by anxieties, the organization man caught in a kind of squirrel-cage feeling of being trapped, a meaninglessness which leaves him a prisoner to himself. On the one hand he is sure that he ought to be free from Communism or from some other demonic force. Yet, more and more he begins to know that he has to be free for something, if he is to know the joy of being free from something.

The Fourth Convention of the Lutheran World Federation confronted the meaning of these tyrannies indicating the self-righteousness of the Communist, the self-righteousness of the humanitarian, the self-righteousness of orthodoxy (making theological dialectics a way of salvation), and the self-righteousness of the activists. All of these must confront the righteousness of God.[5]

The Freedom to Be Called · Perhaps at no point is this sense of freedom better understood than in the sense of the Christian's calling, his vocation as a Christian. In his matchless statement concerning the present power of God, the Holy Spirit, Luther wrote, "I believe that God has called me, as he calls, gathers, enlightens and sanctifies the whole Christian Church on earth." [6] It is this sense of vocation which is the overflow of this sense of freedom. Thus the calling is to be godly, and man is now free to interpret this in the sense of his life and work. The work itself is not the calling. Service is possible in the dimensions of the Church or in any of the areas of man's existence. He may find it easier to express this faith in some places than in others. (Luther believed that it was necessary to have theology and law as a kind of basis for civilization.) But the old line between holy orders and secular orders, between body and spirit, between serving God and serving man was not only ruptured, it was broken down. There is something within us all that doesn't love a wall, especially if that wall is a man-made device to separate us from ourselves and our neighbor because we are separated from our God.

In the terms of his own day, Luther spoke of "The shoemaker or blacksmith" clinging to the Word of faith toward God by which the heart is made clean and to the word of understanding which teaches him how to act toward his neighbor in his station in life. Everything is "Clean to him even if with his hands and his whole body he deals with nothing but dirt." This sense of vocation is increasingly difficult to make clear in a world of urbanization, of automation, of industrialization. It is difficult for the individual to find his sense of calling. Certainly he finds it increasingly complex within the definitions of contemporary industry or society. It is at this place where the discovery of a New Testament concept has new meaning. Man is more than a gear in the machine, or a screw in the gadget. He is a person for whom Christ died. Even his struggle for civil rights is motivated by this fact and faith. By God's grace, this sinful man can know his freedom. Therefore he has a vocation and this calling must be expressed. What a man does in his own house or on the assembly line can be worth as much as if he performed it in heaven. "For what we do in our calling here on earth in accordance with his word and command he counts as if it were done in heaven for him . . . Therefore we should accustom ourselves not to think of our position and work as sacred and well-pleasing to God, not on the occasion of the position and the work, but on account of the word and faith from which the obedience and the work flow. No Christian should despise his position and life if he is living in accordance with the word of God, but should say, 'I believe in Jesus Christ, and do as the Ten Commandments teach, and pray that our Lord God may help me thus to do.' That is a right and holy life, and cannot be made holier even if one fast himself to death." This struggle to know freedom came in the sixteenth century when paying for forgiveness was a financial act, which Roland Bainton calls "the Bingo of the sixteenth century."

However numerous and arduous the vows of the monk and priesthood or the acts of penance by the individual, these works in God's sight are in no way whatever superior to a believing farmer laboring in the field, or a worshipping woman looking after her home. From penance to penitence is a demanding adventure. "Indeed it occurs quite frequently that the common serving man or maid is more acceptable than all the fastings and other works of monks or priests where faith is lacking."

The Dangers of Freedom • This understanding of the freedom that originates from faith has caused all manner of debate. Lutherans loving their faith have found themselves discussing the dimensions of faith with one another. There have been those who asserted that this understanding of the majesty of faith must therefore keep them from association with other Christians. It was not that these others were outside the Christian faith. Discussions concerning lodge memberships and participation in ecumenical affairs which have aired some of the differences between Lutherans only illustrate the common acceptance of a fact. On the one hand there are those who have discovered this freedom to express a faith which must be shared in the whole of society; on the other hand, there are those who believe that it will be diluted or lost if it is not communicated by those who understand. Beyond the differences lies the immediacy of the foundation of freedom. All of these groups are concerned that freedom itself should not be a sentimentalized kind of independence but a logically-originated expression of faith.

At the crux of the matter is the Cross, and at the Cross, the understanding of God's dynamic love. The atonement is the basis for freedom for it is the assurance not just of man's sin but of God's mercy. This is the love that sets a man free. This is the gracious love that is at the heart of his freedom.

"Were the right man not on our side, our striving would be useless." Faith is more than doctrinal assent; an age which scoffs at the fact of God requires the probing for a cross-centered ethic. Wrote Luther from the background of the sixteenth century existence:

Daily we experience how everybody tries to rise above his own level and strives for honor, power, wealth, art, comfortable living and for everything which is big and lofty. Wherever one finds these people, there everybody clings to them, follows them and serves them eagerly. Everybody likes to be there to share in their high standing. On the other hand, nobody likes to look down where poverty, shame, need, misery and fear dwell. Everybody averts the eyes from them. Wherever you find such people, everybody runs away, flees, shies away from them, leaves them. Nobody thinks of helping them and standing by them, to help them to become somebody.[7]

With a few amendments this reads as though it were from the twentieth century. It is in this relationship that the Lutheran Churches of the world have been giving some of their finest thoughts to a re-translation of the concerns of the Gospel to the present problems of vocation. The efforts in Germany, such as the Evangelical Academies, attempt to discover this impact of the Gospel in daily life and the many lay schools of theology which have been sponsored in the United States illustrate this thrust. Once it may have been easy for Christians to say, "Do what Jesus would do." In today's world this understanding becomes more difficult because of the complications of our society. Contemporary man knows that vocation is not limited to the church; he needs to discover that there is a call of God in the whole pattern of life. He finds in Christ the thrust of God toward man; this becomes as meaningful at the panelboard of his jet plane as it does in his relationships with his family.

Freedom is not a revolt against authority. It does revolt against the authority which prevents a man from the free-sharing of this grace of God. It protests setting up anything between a man and God. It rebels against those who would tell him that he must do certain things to win heaven. Yet freedom is a heady thing in itself if it is not rooted in faith. Christian liberty is a theological understanding of freedom which has given both courage and

humility, both judgment and hope to the Christian who
understands. For "faith is a living, active, mighty thing,
so that it is impossible for it not to do good continuously . . . Therefore, man becomes willing and eager
to do good spontaneously, to serve everyone, to suffer all
manner of things for the love of and in praise of God who
has shown man such mercy. Accordingly, it is just as impossible to separate works from faith as it is to sever glowing and burning from fire." [8]

Fellowship · We live in a time which is concerned with
a new exploration of fellowship. It sees the intricate difficulties of gathering together men and women who aren't
righteous in themselves, and binding them into a community which can serve among men. The docking problems of man-made satellites are engineering phenomena;
the relating problems of pardoned men and women who
can act freely as a Christian community are equally intricate. This is grace freely moving among men who discover justification.

It is this understanding which was expressed by the
1963 convention of the Lutheran World Federation:

The church should be nothing other than the steward of the means
by which God justifies the sinner whom he finds both inside and
outside the church. If the church forgets this, it becomes an institution for the cultivation of religious interests or ecclesiastical traditions. It then restricts its effectiveness to certain levels of society and
leads only a ghetto existence . . . Its task is to summon the whole
world, both mankind and the church, before God and proclaim to
both the judgment of God and the justifying verdict.[9]

The fragmentation of life requires a new awareness of
the relevancy of that freedom which grows from the new
being in Christ. "If anyone is in Christ, he is a new creation; the old has passed away, behold the new has come."
(II Cor. 5:17) In the dialogue of our time, this ancient

Christian concept of a responsible freedom that breaks loose from old slaveries, old superstitions, old cultural shackles, needs to be explored. It ought to be a superb contribution of the evangelical witness to the contemporary exploration of the meaning of existence.

The church is not the association of the just but rather the fellowship of "the justified." That idea has been obscured but the theological basis is there. The justifying love of God is known through Word and Sacrament; it is expressed through fellowship and every expression of this love that heals and lifts. This interpretation of Scripture and Christian life, known as justification by faith, is basic to the Lutheran way of life.

V

The Contemporary Voice:
The Word

Lord Keep us steadfast in Thy Word,
Curb those who fain by craft or sword
Would wrest thy Kingdom from Thy Son
And set at naught all He hath done.
—M. Luther

Few subjects have been more full of promise, blessed in understanding, troublesome in discussions and divisive in interpretation than that of the Word of God. For the Lutheran the Word is central. It is pivotal as a major theme running through the life of the church. For Luther this was the climax of his search and all other developments related themselves to the discovery that the Word of God was supreme—not church, or tradition, or any other authority. It is the Bible which he respects so highly at the center of life and so risks everything to translate the Scriptures into the language of the people. This Word is the "norm of faith and life." It is the "manger" for the Christ or the "swaddling clothes" for the Christ, to use Luther's terms. The Church's confessions of faith have value only because they grow out of Scripture.

Think of the Scriptures as the loftiest and noblest of holy things, as the richest of mines, which can never be worked out, so that you may find the wisdom of God that He lays before you in such foolish and simple guise, in order that he may quench all pride. Here you find the swaddling clothes and the manger in which Christ lies, and to which the angel points the shepherds. Simple and little are the swaddling clothes, but dear is the treasure, Christ, that lies in them.[1]

It is in this tradition that Scriptural study becomes the most promising ecumenical adventure today. God the Creator creates and sustains now. God the Saviour redeems and secures men now. God the Holy Spirit calls, gathers and enlightens now. In this unique revelation God confronts man personally. From creation to life eternal, God is the Lord of life and reveals Himself to his People.

Evangelical · Through the centuries the Lutheran family has been known as the Evangelical Lutheran Church, a term indicating essential emphasis on the Scriptures and this certainty of the dynamic Word. Evangelical, or Gospel-centered, became a term in contrast to Church-centered. The good news of the love of God in Christ is the Evangel. The seat of authority was not in an organization or in any other primacy but in the revelation of God captured in the Old and New Testaments, renewed in each generation by the Holy Spirit as the Word is proclaimed. All authority ultimately rests in the "evangel"; hence the church is known as evangelical in its approach, its emphasis and its message. The Gospel is heard through the words, even though to limit the Gospel to the words is to fall into a semantic trap. For the Lutheran, Christ is the Word of God and Christ alone. "This is the true test by which to judge all books, when we see whether they deal with Christ or not, since all the scriptures show us Christ, and St. Paul will know nothing but Christ. What does not teach Christ is not apostolic even though St. Peter or St. Paul taught it; again what preaches Christ would be apostolic even though Judas, Annas, Pilate and Herod did it." [2] So everything in Scripture is to be understood in relation to the center, the message concerning Christ.

This has been a difficult lesson for Lutherans to learn about Lutheranism, yet it is central to an understanding of Christianity if one is to know the living Word of God. For the Word is the living Word, and to imprison the Word in dogma or printed Bible, or in any tradition, is to place the emphasis where it does not belong. "For the word of God is no sleepy wisdom . . . it demonstrates its power in everyone who believes, so he recognizes the gracious God and judges all, comforts some and teaches others." [3] Everything must be understood in relation to the good news of forgiveness.

The Revealed Word • Of all of the subjects discussed by the Lutherans of the world, none has been more intriguing. One can find colloquiums in every language and in current debate all centering in this understanding of the Word. The ancient Councils and the modern higher critics, the learned professors of other centuries and the current discussions of Bultmann's "demytholization," or Cullman's theology are the continuing trail of this exploration. This is an exciting contribution to the present ecumenical discussions maintaining a central stream of influence in the great flowing river of God's revealed Word in the contemporary situation.

There is reason enough to study, explore and treasure the Scriptures. Christ is the living Word and we learn of Him through these Scriptures. And we learn of the Scriptures through Christ. We worship God through this knowledge of the Word and we are led to this understanding of God by the power of the Word. In the Lord's Supper the believing Christian knows the presence in, with and under the Bread and wine; in the Scriptures, the believer knows the real presence of the living Word in, with and under the words. To deify the Bible, is to be subject to idolatry. To ignore the Bible is to miss the revealed word.

Modern Lutherans discovered the full meaning of this

central fact. They have suffered and died for it. They have debated and become divisive because of it. They have witnessed to it; and the proclamation of this Word becomes a priceless privilege. If there has always been the danger that men should attempt to protect the Word, it is in the testing times of war and tyranny that the free flow of the Word and the power of the Word have become clear. For the Word is not in our hands; its communication is ours.

This is a critical issue in our century. We have come to the midway point of the fifth century since the theses were affixed to the door of the church in Wittenberg. Our problem is not translation from one language to another. Our problem is translating into the thought-forms of our age. Luther's translation released the Word into the vernacular of his day. In our century the Word must be released into the vernacular of our contemporary crisis. This is why it requires more than quoting Scripture; it requires an entry into the tensions of today until this living Word is "re-mythologized," thrust into new symbols and continuing links which hold the broken-ness of mankind next to the healing grace of a loving God.

If this is understood, men are free to see the Word alive in the whole of life. It is this free flow of the Word and the lack of fear to examine, to risk and to share as a servant of God, that gives freedom to the mind and incentive to the Spirit. Keeping steadfast in the Word is keeping alive to the living presence of Christ. It is not acting frightened before the assaults of any age. As Luther once vividly wrote, "Wherever you read: He arose, there continue: I with Him, you with Him, so that the resurrection may be drawn into us and we into it. Not to learn this is to learn nothing." [4] For the mighty God is the contemporary God.

The Importance of the Bible · Biblical study is urgently paramount. There are times when the love of the Bible's teachings make Lutherans introspective. It is in the 66 books of the Bible that the historic need for redemption is recognized. The Apocryphal books, between the Old and New Testament are valuable literature, but are not placed in the Canon. It is in this written Word that the reality of forgiveness and the availability of that forgiving love of God to all men is made known. The Bible is revered because it "presses Christ upon the heart." It is through this Bible that we are led to *believe* and to find a sustaining comfort. Here we find the spiritual dimension beyond aspirations. Men have a higher respect for the Bible if they escape the trap of arguing about the size of the whale in the book of Jonah or the height of the gates of pearl. One can confront these events in their proper setting. Here is a rule of norm and faith. One is invited to read the Bible regularly, not to achieve rewards, to hold an amulet in superstitious respect, or to develop a code book of behavior. Have we known the living contemporary Word of God? This is the rockbed of faith which gladly welcomes all scholarly and critical research. "For it is dangerous to play with the Word of God by which conscience and faith are to be guided." Whatever else they do or wherever else they go, Lutherans begin with the Scriptures. Their problem is, sometimes, that they have not soared from this launching pad.

Luther translated the Bible, his German edition becoming an enduring classic. In every country where the Lutheran Church has lived the Bible has come into the language of the people and will continue to do so. The current development of many translations is a logical continuance of this emphasis. Today, scholars continue to work in the field of translation and in all forms of Biblical research. It was a normal act in an abnormal situation of imprisonment that Bishop Berggrav during the Nazi occupation of Norway translated the Scriptures into modern Norwegian. By the same token it ought to be normal

for Lutherans to labor constantly to put their teachings
into the language of the contemporary . . . So Luther
wrote, "In the church we ought to speak as we do at home,
the plain mother tongue, which everyone is acquainted
with. It may be allowed in courtiers, lawyers, advocates,
etc., to use quaint and curious words . . . yet the people
had rather hear a plain brother preach that delivers His
words to their understanding . . . In churches no praising or extolling should be sought after."

The translation never becomes final; it is the living
Word breaking through the translation. In Christ, God is
dealing with mankind, and in Christ we are freed from
the lordship of evil. In the redemptive work and life of
Christ, we find the living Word. This is what is meant
when the Lutheran Church is referred to as Christocentric. It is Christ-centered, and we know this God through
Christ in faith.

Therefore, the Old Testament, the Gospels and the
Epistles of the New Testament, the traditions and doctrines of the Church, the work and life of the Church are
all understood from the central factor that Christ is the
living incarnate Word and through Him, and only through
Him, do we come to know God. Christ is the proclamation
of God and the whole life and work of the Christian must
be this proclamation or witness. The one element by
which the Church lives is the word of God. Scripture must
break into thought forms as well as words. In our Confirmation classes we discovered that very few of these ur-
banized youngsters had ever really known a pasture. How
could they understand the 23rd Psalm? As a result, we had
some of our most creative and exciting sessions "translating" parables of Jesus and familiar passages into contemporary pictures. It hasn't contributed to the literary
heritage of the ages but it was an existential experience
for these young people.

Before this living Word, doctrinal interpretations, tradition and all divisive problems are ultimately subject. The Word of God is and should remain the sole rule and norm of all doctrine, and no human being's writings dare to be put on a par with it, but that everything must be subjected to it. In the contemporary situation the Lutherans of the world have discovered their essential unity which overcomes language or other cultural heritages which had kept them from understanding one another. The matters which the Reformers declared to be secondary in importance are subject to change. As this Gospel is proclaimed and believed and men search for this living Word, there is unity, and such unity should be witnessed to the world and persistently pursued.

It is in this common study that the Christian is strengthened and enabled to live in his present situation. It is in this understanding of the living Word, that the church finds its unity. That unity can be known in a community of respect. It is this common witness to the living Word that we bring into this new era of humanitarian and scientific research, a faith in a living and dynamic God, not in a static God hemmed and hedged. The critical study of Scriptures is not a deterrent but a witness of this dynamic fact. The God who spoke to Abraham, who challenged the prophets, who reconciled mankind through Jesus Christ, who captured the imagination of saints, apostles, martyrs, moves through us and captures our minds and hearts also. That Word of God is not dependent upon the mechanical structure of scripture. As Emil Brunner contends, "The same Spirit that convinced the Apostles, convinces me." [5] There is much hope in the contemporary interest in Scriptural study in the discovery of those factors that will encourage Christian unity.

Communicating the Word · The Lutheran is concerned that God's Word be known and understood, not just canonized. It is the Word—not the church, authority, or the pastor—that becomes the critical issue. Luther once opened a window and strong winds blew through the ancient citadel. His Small Catechism, his Essays and Sermons, his hymns and frequent writings became focal points of continuing Christian Education. The important educational programs in the churches and schools of Europe and the Sunday School teaching in the Western Hemisphere continue to have significance. The average Lutheran Church has a special class taught by the pastor for a period of two or three years before the Rite of Confirmation. The Lutheran dedication to Christian freedom demands this responsible study of the Christian faith. Freedom is not just the liberty to have personal opinions; one does not set himself above the Bible. In the fellowship of the church man finds the discipline of this living Word. Faith was caught but also taught. It was the slow, maturing, growing process that found its expression in home and church and, in those countries where there was a more homogeneous situation, in the school. The encounter between God and man is real but this must be translated, transmitted in the best understanding, using the best methods possible. Christian education does not demand that the growing child give up something in the maturing process, but rather add to it. The work of the Sunday School, and all of the other educational enterprises of the local congregation all share in the important and essential process of growth.

The Preaching of the Word · If this proposition is understood, then the preaching of the Word and the pastoral sermon are not just a matter of "tell me the old, old story"; it is sharing the impact of the old story by modern persons in the modern situation. The sermon is not just the proclamation limited to the pulpit; the purpose in the recounting of the Gospel message is in the faith that this is God's revealed Word for the now. It is this Gospel which gives personal value to this moment. Rooted in Scripture and addressed to the minds of the present, the sermon is the news preached as the public witness of this unfettered Word. It was first incarnate in a time of crisis; it must be a living Word in the present crisis. That kind of evangelical preaching is prophetic.

At a Reformation Service in Buffalo, the stage of the Music Hall had been transformed into the chancel of a church. Seated near the pulpit, I noted that this piece of furniture, which had previously graced a funeral home, still bore the little brass plate "Please Register." Dr. Franklin Clark Fry and I smiled at the caricature. Paradoxically, this is just what the sermon must, and must not do. A sermon registers only when it becomes the way by which the Word of God is laid bare before the mind of the hearer. It does not register if it just brings the name of the preacher to the hearer. Creating a confusion of tongues degrades the preaching. Bonhoeffer once wrote: "At the tower of Babel all the tongues were confounded and as a result men could no longer understand one another as they all spoke different tongues. This confusion is now brought to an end by the language of God, which is universally intelligible and the only means of communicating among men. And the church is the place where that miracle happens." [6] It happens in and through the church if there is the vital character of preaching as the communication of a living word to living people now. The sermon is the focus of the shared witness and as such has validity.

The Reformation restored the sermon to this centrality of the worship service. The sermon is the crossroads of the priestly and the prophetic. It brings the continuity of the heritage into the contemporaneity of the moment. It is the prose of the spoken word that relates the happening of the Gospel, and the poetry of the spoken word that helps men to understand that which they had been seeing. It is the completeness of the Word for the incompleteness of those who assemble to hear. Out of this grows the dialogue. Jesus sent out his disciples to preach, risked the Word in all of the frailties of language and shared in authority through the stumbling, sometimes misunderstood words of people.

Luther was always stating in blunt language his insistence on plainness of speech in preaching:

To preach plain and simply is a great art: Christ himself talks of tilling ground, of mustard seed, etc. He used altogether homely and simple similitudes.

I would not have preachers in their sermons use Hebrew, Greek or foreign languages, for in the church we ought to speak as they are accustomed to do at home, the plain mother tongue, which everyone is acquainted with.

To speak deliberately and slowly best becomes a preacher; for thereby he may the more effectually and impressively deliver his sermon.

Cursed are all preachers that in the church aim at high and hard things and, neglecting the saving health of the poor, unlearned people, seek their own honour and praise, and therewith to please one or two ambitious persons.

When I preach, I sink myself deep down. I regard neither Doctors nor Magistrates of whom are here in this church above forty; but I have an eye to the multitude of young people, children, and servants, of whom there are more than two thousand. I preach to those, directing myself to them that have need thereof. Will not the rest hear me? [7]

The sermon is misunderstood if it is regarded as the only place where the Gospel is communicated. This was never true and it is an absurdity in today's world. The ears are assaulted by verbiage and the mind is cluttered with claims and counterclaims. The sermon is one more pronouncement of God's living presence. It provides a channel of God's word that breathes authority, motivating a hearer into action.

The local parish provides the opportunity for men to hear the words with a marginal or interlinear understanding of the Word. It ought to help men to make up their minds and take sides. It ought to make some men angry and others disturbed. It needs to speak to the diversities of minds and the apartness of so many experiences.

In today's churches the old practice of dialogue is once more assuming its place as a part of the sermon. The chance to think with the pastor about the preached word, provided in the "talk-back" sessions, takes the sermon out of the polite dismissal with, "Nice sermon, Reverend," into the mind-spreading, thought-provoking situation. The Evangelical Academies in Europe and the Faith and Life Institutes in America, which enable professional men and tradesmen to study together, are the direct result of these days when men discovered the meaning of the preached or communicated word.

Philip Schaff in his *History of the Christian Church* stated the case for this proclaimed word in the life of the church in the community:

Under the inspiring influence of the spotless purity of Christ's teaching and example, aided here and there by the noble instincts and tendencies of philosophy, the Christian Church from the beginning asserted the individual rights of man, recognized the divine image in every rational being, taught the common creation and common redemption, the destination of all for immortality and glory, raised the humble and lowly, comforted the prisoner and the captive, the stranger and the exile, proclaimed chastity as a fundamental virtue, elevated woman to the dignity and equality of man, upheld the sanctity and inviolability of the marriage tie, laid the foundation of the Christian family . . . moderated the evils and the underlying foundation of slavery, opposed polygamy and concubinage, emancipated children from the tyrannical control of their parents, made relentless war upon the shocking indecencies of the theater, upon cruelty and oppression and every vice, infused into a heartless and loveless world the spirit of love and brotherhood, transformed sinners into saints, frail women into heroines and lit up the darkness of the tomb by the ray of unending bliss in Heaven.[8]

That happens over and over again when the Word is shared. Then a person—or a community of persons—is changed, not only by the preacher or the layman but by the compelling spirit of the living God. This is the essential genius of the Christian community, and it is this witness, alive and alert in today's world, relevant to today's situations, concerned with today's problems, and communicated by today's people which is the *Now* in *Eternity*. This relevant Word so understands the Eternal Truth as it confronts the present dilemma.

This was also true in Luther's day. There is in his writings the constant reiteration of the evangelical witness—the sense of God's disclosure—which erupts and breaks loose:

And it, the Gospel, really is not what you find in the books and what is contained in the letters, but rather a spoken declaration and living Word—a voice which responds, is publicly proclaimed, and everywhere heard . . . Therefore if one would ask what the Gospel is, the sophists of the higher schools would answer: it is a book which teaches a good thing. They do not know what because they do not understand it. Gospel means a good message.[9]

Not all apostles wrote . . . and even those who did write did nothing more than direct us into the old Scriptures. Just as the angel directed the shepherds to the manger and the diapers! Therefore it is not all according to the New Testament to write books about Christ's teaching—but there should, instead of books, be in all places good, learned, zealous and devout preachers who draw the living Word out of the old writings, and constantly nurture the people as the apostles had done. Before they wrote they had preached to the people with bodily voice and converted them, which was their specifically apostolic and New Testament work.[10]

As K. E. Skydsgaard insists:

When Luther says that the Church is not a "Pen house" but a "Mouth house," he is referring to the mystery which lies in the hearing of God's word for salvation. It is always a human word—how could it be otherwise—but a human word which the living God takes unto himself and expresses as his own. It is true now as well as in the time of Jesus: He who has ears to hear, let him hear. The word can lie dead upon the lips of men, pale as a corpse; but it can also become the residence of the Spirit and its power and ignite so that the tongues are aflame.[11]

So the problem of sharing the Word of God is more than language. It is, as Grady Davis insists, "a very old problem; eyes that see not and ears that hear not because the heart, having let go of nature, no longer has a vocabulary of workable images in which to recognize and through which to share its deep realities. I think the debased currency of contemporary speech is the direct result of bankrupt hearts, bankrupt because cut off from their sources of supply in nature." [12]

We know the Real Presence in the Word and Sacrament; that needs to be understood in the contemporary situation, in the spoken word and in the shared teaching, in the gathered congregation and in the sensitive community. It requires that we go all the way for, as Luther said, "Scripture begins tenderly and leads us to Christ as a man, then to the Lord over all the creatures and then to God." [13] Lutheranism is Evangelical, loving the Gospel, and, at its best, translating Christian truth in the exciting semantics of this time of change.

VI

The Hinges of Grace:
The Sacraments

Then let us feast this Easter Day
On the true bread of heaven;
The Word of grace hath purged away
The old and wicked leaven;
Christ alone our souls will feed
He is our meat and drink indeed,
Faith lives upon no other! Alleluia!
—*M. Luther*

Means of Grace · To ignore formulation of meaning in discussing mystery is to risk its presence as superstition. To limit mystery to formula is to miss its meaning. It is the treading of the difficult but challenging edge between these two facts that marks Lutheranism's understanding of the Sacraments. There are many holy rites of the Church such as Confirmation, Ordination and Marriage. Beyond these are two sacraments, marking a deliberate act by the believer and a deliberate act by God meeting in this center of action. Here is an authentic witness of the Presence of Christ. These are among the visible marks of the living church. This concept of the sacrament demands more than reason but not less than reason. It asks a believer to think to the ends of his ability and yet insists that there is more beyond. So the Word is known in Scripture and in Sacraments. To put it another way, whereas the Roman

Catholic may think of the mystery of the sacrament as solely God's act (the physical miracle), and many Protestants may think of the sacrament as man's memorial to an act of God (the spiritual miracle), the Lutheran considers the sacrament as the meeting place of both actions.

Luther struggled with words at this point insisting that the body and blood of Christ were "in, with, and under" the bread and wine or that the water of baptism has significance only as "comprehended in God's command and connected with God's word." These are more than semantic exercises, for one soon discovers the problem of putting dimensions around that which cannot be measured. One cannot fully comprehend the meaning of Christ Himself, yet it is possible to know Him as the Word become flesh. He was a definite person, living at a definite time in a definite place. This definiteness only serves to illustrate the divine quality which outleaps the physical form and makes Christ the Lord and Saviour of all mankind, in every age, in every place. The Sacrament is the constant illustration of this fact.

More than Ceremony • The age in which we live has a tendency to bludgeon its way through symbols in its concern with materialism and pragmatism, either by misunderstanding or by forgetting the meaning of the symbol. Every advance in this time of storm and stress underscores the importance of the symbol. This is never more clear than when man attempts to reach beyond his own social, racial or personal situation. Then the symbol outstrips language and reaches through the differences while still admitting them.

The ultimate purpose of the Sacrament, an act instituted by Christ Himself, is not to have a ceremony which somehow emotionally ties people into a fellowship. This is only a by-product. The communion is with God. This is man's leap toward God and God's meeting of man. Whenever the Sacrament is regarded as only a ceremony of the church, it is in danger of becoming either useless as a sentimentality or divisive because of mechanical technicalities. Here in the sacraments, earthly materials such as water, bread and wine are used in the full knowledge that they remain earthly materials and only have meaning in the connection with the understanding of the Word of God. By "the Word," the Lutheran means God's continuing activity. There is a real presence.

This fact has caused many discussions by those who care deeply that the purity of the sacrament be preserved. Lutherans continue to have their full measure of these discussions. Where the sacraments should unite, they have often seemed to divide. On one thing Lutherans are agreed; namely, that these elements are valid as they are understood in the context of the Word of God and are effective since they were established by Christ. The fellowship is the communion of believers. This loving act of God is concerned not just with holy things but with a holy deed. This is the communion showing "the Lord's death until He come," the corporate act of praise in the recognition of His living presence.

The Reason for the Deed • There would be little reason for this idea of the sacrament unless there is a need to understand God's love and forgiveness. Deep at the heart of Lutheran theology is a pessimism about man and an optimism about God. The sinfulness of man is no little mistake or misjudgment. Sin is at the very heart of man with his estrangement from God and so from himself. Original sin is no empty doctrine; it is the understanding of man's helplessness before the fact of his own salvation. Any "pull yourself up by your own bootstrap" or "get ahead by conforming to the crowd" or "achieve your height by thinking tall" is lost before the reality itself.

In this struggle Christ becomes God's deed. It is not only in what Jesus does, or says. It is in what He is. The fact of His being which involves life and His death on the cross, are the stopping of the pull downward. "God was in Christ reconciling the world unto Himself." (2 Cor. 5:19)

The forgiving love of God which always is stretched toward man is now known, understood and revealed in the life of Christ. The penitent know the grace of God at the heart of the sacrament. This act of the church is the witness to this act of God. These visible signs of inward and spiritual grace are physical acts as the life of Christ is a physical fact. Thus the love of God is in history but it is not limited to history. The physical signs such as water and bread and wine, are the elements but they are not the thing itself. It is the love of God that is basic and it is the knowing of this love that is shared in the constant renewal of the act of forgiving love which we know through the Word and the Sacraments.

Much of man's sense of guilt and his inability to deal with his frustrations stems from a concern with himself and his comforts. He is lost in the present with no sense of power beyond himself that will enable him to live with himself. At this point, sacramentalism is not dead magic or habitual formalism. But life need not be intolerable in any age. The words of faith, hope and love must be reinterpreted in every time and in every situation. It is our dilemma that while we may fail to find strength beyond ourselves, we are at the same time sending our frail selves out into space. The littleness of man, which Kierkegaard once typified as swimming in waters 70,000 fathoms deep, can also sense the reality of God's presence when he is out of his depth. To share in the Sacraments is to acknowledge the presence of God in any situation. The power that

ministers through frail symbols can also motivate these
fragile forms of life here or in space.

Baptism • There is a classic definition in *Luther's Catechism* as he describes baptism as not simply water but the
water comprehended in God's command and connected
with God's Word, water used together with God's Word
and by His command. His love is not dependent upon intellectual comprehension. It is God's act. It is the clear
sign of God's gift of grace. This ancient ceremony
achieves new meaning in the life and act of Jesus Christ
becoming the Word of God in action in this moment.
God the Creator made this universe. God the Christ is
the revelation of God's forgiving salvation in this universe.
Now the continuing love of God, the Holy Spirit, speaks
in and through these acts, expressing a kind of official seal
for the act. Whether it is a newborn baby or an adult,
baptism expresses the purifying love of God. Here the
Lutheran is not so concerned with method, the amount of
water used, the mechanics of administration or the age of
the person receiving baptism. He is concerned with the
fact that moves in and through the water. The Sacrament
is the act of God, administered by the church; beyond this
is its expression in the life of the believer. So to be baptized is to know that one has been deliberately placed
either as an infant or as an adult within the climate or
environment of the church; beyond this the believer himself expresses the result of this encouraging climate.

This means that the Sacrament of Baptism administered
in any Christian Church acknowledging this lordship of
Christ is acceptable. A Roman Catholic, uniting with the
Lutheran Church, would not have to be, nor should be,
rebaptized. This would be an affront as baptism is generally recognized now in all Christian Churches, Protestant and Roman Catholic.

The Child · Since baptism has been shared with infants, there is also the need to grow in this grace. Grace is not static and the act of baptism is not an irrevocable act which insulates a child from evil, as the dipping of Achilles was supposed to do. The child can undo that which is done for him; the person can behave as though this act never took place.

At the baptism of the infant there are sponsors, once known as "Godparents." Too frequently these are but honorary offices in today's practice. The sponsor is meant to be a spiritual assistant in the rearing of the child. The sponsor is to assist in creating the environment for the development of a maturing faith. Then, at the age of 12–15 years the child witnesses to his faith in a new and personal way—Confirmation.

Confirmation · Lutheranism has universally shared in the rite of confirmation usually following a period of two or three years of education and guidance under the tutelage of the pastor. Because of the varieties of situations in which the Lutheran Church finds itself, this training period varies both in its number of years and also as far as the ages of the young people are concerned. On the whole, most churches in the Western Hemisphere confirm upon the entrance into high school or at about the 14th or 15th year.

At this point Lutherans have certain traditions but they are not bound by them. Usually the baptized child, growing up in the church, attending the services of worship and now particularly schooled in the essentials of his faith is introduced into the regular active membership of the congregation by confirmation. He then participates in the Sacrament of the Lord's Supper. This is the tradition. There are a few Lutherans who admit a child to the Sacra-

ment of the Lord's Supper before confirmation, and bring
the age of confirmation to 18 years or older. The whole
subject of confirmation is being vigorously rethought in
contemporary society.

Whenever or however the act of confirmation takes
place, it is both an intellectual and emotional event which
enables a person to identify his Christian experience with
that Prayer of Confirmation: "To thy strengthening in
faith, to thy growth in grace, to thy patience in suffering
and to the blessed hope of everlasting life."

In adolescence there is a specific renewal of baptism, a
validating of a fact by giving this experience a new intellectual awareness and an emotional significance which
baptism requires. In one connection Luther asked for a
daily baptism, not in the sense of the sacrament, but in
the sense of daily renewal of the fact of man's entrance
into a knowledge of God's love. Confirmation underscores
this need. Baptism and confirmation are growth in grace!

The Lord's Supper • Known variously as *The Lord's Supper, Last Supper, Holy Communion, Sacrament of the
Altar* or the *Eucharist,* this Sacrament of the church is
the constant renewal of the awareness of God's love. Begun in the celebration of the ancient Jewish Passover—
filled with a new and revolutionary meaning in the fact of
the Cross, probed thoroughly by Christians as they have
tried to find the meanings of its mystery—it is today a
significant vessel or channel by which the love of God is
known. Just as the Word, to which man owes his faith, is
not just in artificial hearing, so the justification of the
Sacraments is not limited to formal participation. These
forms were always invested with meaning, and they are
valid today in this same manner. Whenever the ceremonial
side of the act is bogged down in determining the method
of administration there is the danger of missing the con-

stant renewal inherent in the reason for the Sacrament. Always it is only where communion with Christ is a reality that the ceremony, the act and the witness are validated.

In practice, the Lutheran refers to the Lord's Supper as *The Sacrament of the Altar*. He is accustomed to come to the altar, to receive both the unleavened bread and the wine and to hear there the words, "The body and blood of our Lord Jesus, strengthen you and keep you in true faith unto everlasting life." There are varieties in the practice but the diversities are within the general pattern. Sometimes the common chalice is used; more often the individual cup is the practice. Liturgical renewal is bringing a rethinking of the forms and customs of the service; the heart of the matter is still the sharing in the Real Presence.

His body is not in a distant heaven up to which a man must swing himself on the wings of faith. He is in the sacrament itself, upon the earth, in the "mediated immediacy" of the Word of God connected with the bread and wine and the bodily eating and drinking. Here we should think of wholes; and it is important not to exclude the body, for this would exclude part of the creation Christ came to redeem and with which he himself was united. The presence of Christ is therefore a presence of the total Christ.[1]

Confession • The observance of private or public confession has been and still is a practice of the Lutheran Church. If Holy Communion is to be both hallowed in fact and in participation, it must be more than a nice thing to do. It is the recognition of how much of daily life is unhallowed and lacking in participation in the work of the Kingdom. Confession is private—the personal examination and admission, and public—as the congregation kneels in common witness of its common sin. Honesty in the church adds new meaning to this act. Social conflicts demand regular understanding of confession or one of the basic understandings of forgiveness and redemption is lost to the Christian experience.

Public confession is a part of every regular service of worship in the Lutheran tradition. The words in the liturgy call the worshippers to confess:

Almighty God, our Maker and Redeemer, we poor sinners confess unto Thee that we have sinned against Thee by thought, word and deed. Wherefore we flee for refuge to Thine infinite mercy, seeking and imploring Thy grace for the sake of our Lord Jesus Christ.

This common statement brings into one prayer the particular and the specific. The problem for the contemporary man is that he may not feel either the depths of sin or the heights of grace. Confession can be private, as indeed it is in many instances when in the certainty of confidentiality the parishioner and pastor—or member with member —lay bare the problem and seek the healing grace. The problem of the private confessional is that it becomes too particularized, a focus on one event or attitude to the neglect of the whole. The problem of public confession is that it is so general and familiar that it can become only a repetition of words.

A young man recently suggested that there is not the quality of honesty in the church that one should expect. His listeners looked shocked but then admitted that the church can unwittingly provide a facade of respectability which provides a retreat from honesty.

The Psalmist said, "My cup runneth over." (Psalm 23) Confession is the removal of a lid from the cup so that the grace of God can be poured in. That confession is not an act of virtue. It is the response of the worshipper to the love of God. Confession is the prayer:

Create in me a clean heart, O God, and renew a right spirit within me.

Cast me not away from thy presence and take not thy Holy Spirit from me.

Restore to me the joy of thy salvation, and uphold me with thy free spirit. (Psalm 51)

Confession is the admission of the involvement of each person in the woundings of life, ranging from omission to commission, from apathy to deliberate insulation of spirit, from ignorance of hurts because we can travel so rapidly to an ignorance of social evil because we live so selfishly.

Luther protested against this enumeration of sins, as constituting act of righteousness. The contemporary Lutheran protests the mediocrity of faith which equates religion with ethnic or political virtues, thus putting the lid on the cup. We are still "sinners standing in the need of grace." Helmut Thielicke has written that "We have gradually become accustomed to the dangerous and unhealthy idea that the Grace of God is thrown at us. Perhaps God has first to be jerked from us complacent western Christians, like a rug from under our feet, if we are to be awakened to this surprise." [2]

The Real Presence • As Christians have tried to discover the dimensions of the Sacrament of the Lord's Supper they have stated the case in varying ways. The Roman Catholic speaks of transubstantiation or the physical miracle of the Mass in which the bread and the wine become the actual body and blood of Jesus. This concept of the Host is the physical extreme of a devotional concept of the mystery of the Event.

Some Protestants have regarded the Sacrament only as a memorial, since Christ himself said: "this do in remembrance of me." (Luke 22:19) Thus the commemorative meal becomes a way in which the historic act is renewed in the minds of the believer.

For the Lutheran the Lord's Supper is the Real Presence, the understanding of Christ's contemporary power, of the Holy Spirit's living act, of God's present concern. The bread is still bread but something happens here beside the remembrance of the fact. The Real Presence is discerned only in faith. Alone, the bread and wine are an absurdity; with the Word they become the vehicles of grace.

At the risk of the weakness of any illustration the case may be stated in this simple form. I have a friend who lives in a certain house. The Roman Catholic may believe that the house has become so invested with the person that in the holy act of the church, the house and the person are identified. The symbolical view is that every time I pass that house I think of the person who lives there. The Lutheran says that the house and the person are different, and yet, when I share in the sacrament I have knocked at the door (the act of the church) and the door has been opened (the act of God) and there Christ meets me. There is no confusion between the house and the person and this person is known in other ways than by the involvement with the house. Yet I find this meeting with him in a particular and specific way which is understood beyond class, caste, language and varieties of mankind. In the contemporary dialogue it is apparent that the concept of the Real Presence is an ecumenical crossroad where fellow-Christians, beyond their official confessional statements, are meeting. It is obvious that when Roman Catholic and Protestant go beyond semantic patterns and describe their understanding of the sacramental experience, they may meet in a common understanding.

Open and Closed Communion • There has been a very real consciousness among Lutherans of the words of Scripture which indicate that a man can eat and drink to his own condemnation. The early church was concerned with romanticizing the Sacrament. In the context of our present world, we still have this sentimental danger. On one side there are Lutherans who have insisted that there ought to be a knowledge of communion with God—thus a doctrinal oneness which can best be known by actual sharing in the life of the congregation. The worshipper is known to the pastor; there is a discipline involved in this sharing in the Lord's Supper. In this sense, it is closed communion, limiting the participation to those who are the members of that congregation or of that denominational group.

On the other hand there are other Lutherans who testify as vigorously for the same purity of practice and doctrinal concern, placing the emphasis not in the formal membership of that congregation but in the confession of faith of the worshipper. In this praying, witnessing fellowship each worshipper confesses his need of God's love, his faith in God's presence, and his involvement in the total arena of life. Communion is not a willy-nilly inviting in of anyone, but an invitation to all who thus confess that God's grace is involved. The legalism of the administration is removed by the understanding of the grace of God. These varieties of administration are all-too-often the divisive elements which distort the whole meaning of the Sacrament and deliver it into what modern observers have called a "scandal." Scandals they may be, but scandals are not overcome by ignoring them. Nor are they banished by constant involvement in a history class which is only concerned with how the scandal came to be. The dilemma is overcome by a loving awareness that the grace of God is coming to us in this shared, worshipping fellowship and it must be understood in this context as well as in relationship to our own situation now. It isn't a matter of deciding who is right; it is realizing that all men need to understand the righteous love of God. Just as to forgive means to restore, so in our very hush before the awesome love of God, there can be the understanding of this precious and continuing renewal of life. For "the forgiveness of sins, life and salvation are given to us in the Sacrament."

After the Sacraments, What? • In a sense, there is no "after the sacraments." There is something that follows the administration of the sacraments but for Luther and his followers this is but the focus of the constant act. The sacraments are not obligatory festivals nor automatic pieties but the understanding of the involvement of the love of God in the total arena of life. If simple forms of bread and wine and water can be understood and connected with the Word of God, in like manner the whole of life is connected with this Word. Then all bread and the complex significance of bread are connected. Lutherans have had to understand how this fact outleaps their cultural concern (language and customs) and know too, the requirement of overcoming the political barriers which have disturbed life. Sometimes it is the Communist, that enemy of the Christian, who understands this better than the believer. If the Communist forbids the East Zone worshipper from attending the Kirchentag, this tyranny is a kind of recognition of a way of life which many a worshipper in the more calm and prosaic areas of the world has missed. It would be a tragedy if our martyrdoms were only at the political level and not at the religious level. As Gerhard Ebling has written, "worldly talk of God is godly talk of the world." [3]

In Baptism and the Lord's Supper, the Christian discovers a focus of the love of God in a special way and he witnesses to this love in the redemptive follow-through in his own life. The scandal of the sacraments is not limited to varieties of administration but is also apparent in these vital events which limits them to the church instead of understanding the redemptive love of God in the slums, in the racial divisions, or in the understanding of the horror of the evil that makes puppets of men's souls. A man who goes to the Altar to share in the redemptive focus and feels no urgency to bring this same redeeming healing into the relations of mankind "eats and drinks unworthily." [4] It is no idle thing to remember that Judas was at the Last Supper. It is no idle thing to sense the faith of the believer in understanding this meeting of forgiveness and evil, of love and hatred, of truth and untruth which are always gathered at the Cross.

The forms of the Sacraments have varied from age to age; the essential meaning has remained vital. Luther spoke of the sacraments as the summary of the Gospel. Here Christ meets the believer; here is the motive and the power for the believer to meet his neighbor. The sacramental is focused at font and altar; it is shared in the continuing remembrance of His Real Presence. He is "in, with and under" water, the bread and the wine; this same Christ is 'in, with and under' the whole experience of life.

As Lutherans confront this precious heritage and their own unhappy divisions they need to confess as a body of Christians, to receive this same healing grace and become the powerful bearers of the Word. It is not a time that permits isolation from one another. That has been the insistence of the grace of God. It is now the urgent obligation to the world in which we live.

VII

The Priesthood of Believers:
Vocation

Come, Holy Spirit, God and Lord;
Be all thy gifts in plenty poured
To save, to strengthen and make whole
Each ready mind, each waiting soul.
O by the brightness of thy light
In holy faith all men unite,
And to thy praise, by every tongue
In every land, our hymn be sung. Alleluia, Alleluia.
　　　　　　　　　　　　　　—M. Luther

Priests • To comprehend a motivating drive of true Christian fellowship is to understand the meaning of the priesthood of believers. The Lutheran is certain that God's grace is available to all. In this sense the believer is also a priest. That priesthood is not a self-aggrandizement. He is not just a priest within himself. He is a priest to his neighbor. That's the motivation which makes him a burning social conscience and not a slave of an institution. He finds in this fact that nothing in any institution or in the pretenses of any individual can stand between God and him. Neither can these stand between him and his neighbor. He has the right to believe; he has the obligation to share that belief. He has that understanding of God's love which binds him to God; he has that binding to his neighbor because of the same love.

This was revolutionary in other periods of history and it becomes a basic factor to be kept in communication in a time when it is so easy to make religion the possession of the professional churchman or the institutions. "Here is the secret of Martin Luther. He knew that to understand any teaching, any sphere of life, one must enter into it, accept it as one's calling." [1]

The discovery that we are priests brings grace into a new relationship and leads to an understanding of a man's calling. This could be the motivation of a new social revolution in Christian thinking and behavior.

As we have seen previously, his *beruf*, his vocation or his calling is not to a sacred office within the church. The fact that Luther understood clearly was that the church of his day was divided, split between clergy and laity. It was separated not vertically in denominations but horizontally between the sacred and the secular. It was this split that he protested. It was his insistence that God makes his own witness in the world and doesn't need the clergy, the holy offices, or the institutionalism of the church to make it valid. Institutionalism can be the necessary servant and important tool but it is not the substitute for that *beruf*. Man is called by the grace of God to be godly; to pretend that God's call is involved only in certain dimensioned professions is to perpetrate a ghastly heresy. It is this rashness that has enabled men, in the name of God, to press their own conceits upon their brothers and to do it in the name of faith, the church, or God! It is this understanding of the New Testament that has shocked the rigidities of an age which had hardened clerical forms into the pretense of a sole receptacle for godly vocation.

Vocation: • Vocation has received further challenge in the twentieth century. When men can seriously contemplate 27-hour work weeks and retirement at the age of 50, there needs to be a new understanding about the very nature of man and his rights and obligations. He must rethink his purpose in life. The fearful unbalance of wealth —millions are underfed while more than a billion dollars is spent annually on pets—insists that there be another concept of the nature of man's calling. Are we just to devour, to enjoy, to nurse our own selves and our whims, or are we called for another purpose? Are we called to despoil our natural resources and pollute the water and air? "What is man that thou art mindful of him?" (Psalm 8:4) Are we to enjoy life or to exploit it and abuse it?

All of this has become paramount in the continuing development of an understanding of the priesthood of believers. It has pursued the possibilities of the relationship between faith and daily work in dramatic conferences; now the time has come for a thoughtful expression of this understanding of vocation as a continuing Reformation. These are efforts to explore the Lutheran insistence of the priesthood of his faith in the whole of life. A leader in the development of such conferences has stated: "The great challenge before the church is to be the church in the secular involvement in which it is already engaged. The really critical and neglected frontiers of stewardship are less in the organized life of the church than in the institutions and structures of society. If racial tensions at home and abroad should erupt into race war and ideological conflict or blind nationalism should engulf the world in atomic holocaust, it will not be because our Sunday School enrollment was not large enough or we didn't organize enough new congregations, but because this age failed in racial justice and could not manage the problems of wealth versus poverty."

These become the modern expressions of Luther's insistence that the Christian calling was not to be dimensional.

All our work in the field, in the garden, in the city, in the home, in struggle, in government—to what does it all amount before God except child's play, by means of which God is pleased to give his gifts in the field, at home and everywhere? These are the masks of our Lord God, behind which he wants to be hidden and do all things . . . God bestows all that is good on us, but you must stretch out your hands and take hold of the horns of the bull. You must work and lend yourself as a man and a mask to God.[2]

Man is not inhibited by trying to please God by his little acts; he is free from this kind of prideful heresy and free for that humble service in which he prays that the "will of God be done, even through us."

Roland Bainton has summarized this Lutheran contribution to vocation.

The term "vocation" was transferred by Luther from the cloister to the workshop. The expression "vocational guidance" in its modern usage stems directly from him. In his eyes the occupations of the farmer, the doctor, the school teacher, the minister, the magistrate, the housemother, the maidservant and the manservant were all of them religious callings, vocations in which one was bound to render no lip service but to work diligently as serving not merely an earthly but a heavenly master. The net result was to produce a morale for industry, not any fury of work, nor any disparagement of diversion, but a sense of duty in giving an honest day's toil. This attitude readily carried over from farm to factory and provided the entrepreneur with productive wage earners.[3]

The Two Kingdoms • The priesthood of believers is not a static concept. It is the crossroads of the Christian fact and the Christian faith. To the Lutheran there are two kingdoms, one in heaven and one on earth but God is the ruler of both. Since this is true, then pastors and rulers are God's servants. Paul had spoken of the children of Adam and the children of Christ (Romans 5) and Luther also spoke of this in his particular age, which was different in form and concept from the twentieth century. Extremists have taken this idea and used it as a form of escape instead of a form of contact. There have been those who accused Luther of advocating a retreat from tackling the issues of the state, thus preparing the way for a Hitler. Nothing could be farther from the truth.

For Luther, the ruler can be the servant of God just as the clergy can be the servant of God. Man is not to endure the ruler, or just to accept the presence of evil. A hostile ruler or a dictator enslaving the minds of men is to be resisted, just as the hostility of a church is to be resisted. So he could write,

> Though devils all the world should fill,
> All watching to devour us,
> We tremble not, we fear no ill,
> They cannot overpower us.

In the time of the Reformation, the Church insisted on ruling the State. Luther protested this heresy insisting that God is not speaking in and through the organized church alone. He thought of the State as divinely ordained, orderly government creating the environment for the free expression of the love of God.

It is this idea which was distorted into apathy on one hand or into a split-personality on the other, so men could tolerate inhumanities and believe that they were obeying the State. It took the rude shock and horror of World War II to reveal the madness of this distortion. We are all too willing to pass by on the other side as Jesus said in the Parable of the Good Samaritan.

It is not a Lutheran doctrine that the State is to be obeyed blindly. It is a Lutheran doctrine that God speaks in and through the whole of his creation.

Social Environment • Another area of difficulty arising out of the same dilemma has been the concept that the priesthood of believers somehow precludes a social salvation. The focus has been on the individual, the knowledge that the trouble is not in the environment but in man himself. Where one draws the line between individual and social is not a definite demarcation; it is as hazy as the lines between church and state.

There has been a cautiousness about equating bold social experiments with the work of the kingdom but that ought not to discourage the meaning of the experiment. Lutherans have had some embarrassing moments in history, when they were not only cautious but downright hostile to these experiments. In recent years the very presence of tyrannical despots and the equally dangerous ugliness of racial bigotries and economic divisiveness underscored the obvious. God is the ruler of both kingdoms. That's what Luther had said. Unhappy division between sacred and secular brought men into a shambles that ranged from anti-Semitism in some areas to social apathy in others. These "kingdoms" are not separated; they are opposite sides of the same coin. This becomes agonizingly important as the powers for total destruction become more apparent. The derangement of man can cause a total destruction, thus becoming the dangerous caricature of the ancient problem of "Am I my brother's keeper?" Dr. Edgar Carlson has underscored the problem, "If the church at all levels can be given to understand what its responsibility is in relation to the secular order, and implement that understanding with the appropriate witness both to individuals and to governments, it will have gone far toward realizing its mission in a world where actual and potential tragedy is of such dimensions as to stagger the mind and imagination of man." [4]

The Community of Believers • This priesthood is not a group of pious Christians, withdrawn from the world. It is here that the Lutheran Christian has felt a tension as he confronts the tyrannies of the world, knowing how impossible it is to please God by building a social order or an ecclesiastical foxhole. He confronts the tension that there is no church or priest standing between the individual and his Lord. There is no monastery or church or pious activity which can serve as a place of withdrawal from this world. By the same token, God speaks within the monastery or the church. Furthermore, if God is the God of all, then there is *no* work or job that is outside the sovereignty of God. In this sense, the Lutheran Way of Life is confronting the whole of life as a servant of God as he is known through Jesus Christ.

It would be so much easier for these "priests" of the Christian way of life if there were some orderly rules, codes of discipline, or more specific ways which would state, in precise definitions, what one could or could not do. Yet the community of believers is set in the world and the twentieth century has only heightened the tension. What can this community do?

At this point, the Lutheran contribution to today's situation is once more to insist that no political situation can be the final parallel to the kingdom of God. It isn't as easy as that. It is also necessary to reiterate its own principles, that as men express the love of God that they have known through Christ, they find the way to work out ethical principles, racial tensions and political realities. The very social and economic existence of the twentieth century demand that this priesthood of believers not be a withdrawn company, but a channel of God's grace. This Luther envisioned even though he could not have imagined the modern world.

Either the Christian community serves as a leaven and light in the world or it loses its right, as well as its opportunity, for existence. We cannot be personally pious and wink at racial injustice. We cannot be theologically precise and ignore political tyrannies. By his very statements of faith, a Lutheran cannot be devotionally correct and withdraw from the agonies of the neighborhood. He blasphemes if he cynically prays for that which he has no intention of emulating. The very concept of the priesthood of believers demands that the Christian shall be passionately concerned, not because there is a natural order of creation but because there is a will of God to be known in every situation which calls, gathers, enlightens and sanctifies the whole Christian Church on earth. Twentieth century Lutherans have been brought face to face with the terrible urgencies of standing against certain political facts as have Bonhoeffer, Kaj Munk, Niemoller, Lilje, Bishop Dibelius and a countless number of other heroes who have witnessed against communism and fascism in various places of the world. For most of us it is not the political dictation but the tyranny of the local community or our own confusion that defeats vocation. As Richard Luecke has underscored, "Faith requires not only the obedience but the appreciation of the moment. Those who play well, work well; and those who live well, die well. The trouble with most men is that they work while they play and play while they work, and know neither how to live nor how to die." [5]

So each body of Christian men and women not only stand against these acts of sin but they stand for certain community behavior. They are not only Protestants in the sense of protesters. They are Protestants not because they stand against certain things. They are Protestants because they are prophetic Christians, boldly standing for principles of righteousness, even when they know that those acts in themselves can no more save them than they could when St. Paul proclaimed that neither burning at the stake nor giving one's life could overcome the love of God.

Lutheran Men and Women · The work of the church is not committed to clergymen. It is the witness of men and women who have a Christian commitment, who are not disengaged from the world, denouncing that world as alien, but understanding it better than the secularist. To adequately tell of the life of Lutheranism is to recount the stories of the influence of men in the whole of society as well as in their devoted leadership in the local congregation. It is to tell of the leadership of women in the total life of the community, not only in the exciting programs of their church-related activities.

Chief among its influences is a theological emphasis upon the dignity and worth of the ministry of the laity. That is known in the life and program of the church but it is best known in its sharing in the nonchurch groups.

Now the Roman Catholic Church has added its witness to this fundamental understanding of the laity of the church in this urgent witness to the world. Christian vocation may be expressed through the structures of the church; it is certainly expressed in this Christian witness in the world of economics, in politics, in the social structures of mankind. These are the exciting days when believers renew their understanding of this priesthood of believers.

This involves continuing education. It involves new research and a re-examination of Luther's insistence that the form of the institution must assist, not hinder, the sharing of the Christian witness to the world. The Lutheran way of life brought this influence into the dialogue; now it is called to renew and rethink this fundamental understanding of the calling of the Christian person. In strange new ways, men must understand what it means to live fully in this world and to know what it means to say, "Here I stand, I can do no other. God help me."

VIII

The Household of Faith:
The Church

Did we in our own strength confide
Our striving would be losing
Were not the right Man on our side,
The Man of God's own choosing.
Dost ask who that may be?
Christ Jesus it is he;
Lord Sabbaoth his name
From age to age the same
And he must win the battle.
—M. Luther

"There was a time to divide; now there is a time to unite." This frequently-reiterated statement is a call for doctrinal understanding and faithful action. There is a climate for each "getting together" and these are the decades which strengthen that desire. The prayer of Jesus "that they may be one" (John 17:20, 21) has been variously interpreted and yet from Roman Catholic, Orthodox and Protestant groups, comes the insistent desire for the unity of the church. This has been historically basic in Lutheranism.

If Lutherans have ever been separatist or divisive, they have been so in attempting to be true to their own confessions. They have been concerned that the Gospel be rightly preached and the Sacraments administered for all people. This same concern now takes them into ecumenical discussion and common work. As Luther himself wrote, "It is a great consolation that he will make his abode with us. Where God is, there is his temple. God's abode is where he speaks, works and is found. This occurs in a Christian man, and nothing is more precious." Likewise he spoke of the community or communion of Christians, helping men to understand it as that gathering together of believers, those who knew of their justification by faith, and their binding tie in a congregation. The church was not and is not just a collection of persons or an audience. It is a communion, a congregation held together not by culture, economics, language or race, but by the grace of God living in their hearts and binding them beyond these man-made or artificial barriers. Thus the Lutheran ecclesiological concept demands continuing confessional study. This is the ideal. Lutherans haven't always lived up to it, yet this is the common confession of faith. Lutheranism teaches a community of believers (congregation) not an exclusive club (segregation). This all Lutheran groups have confessed.

When Jesus spoke to his disciples concerning their relationship to the power of God, he portrayed it in terms of a vine and branches. It was this close livingness that typified the church. Later, when Paul speaks of the church, he refers to it as a building, but it is a living building in which the believers fit together, growing together. The building is an architectural triumph not because of artificially-gathered stones, but because of the remarkable way in which its stones and lines move together.

This ideal is overshadowed by the physical side of the church. Just as the soul is the important essence of man, still "we are to present our bodies which is a reasonable service." (Romans 12:1 ff.) By the same token it is the communion of believers, held by the very life of Christ which is the essence of the church but that church is known through the physical forms and activities. The Church is the instrument of God's work. It is this Church, already in existence, that can state its faith. As a physical organization it becomes secularized; as a spiritual organization it is the recognition of the lordship of Christ over a company of believers as well as the individual. It is dynamic, always reforming and being reformed, changing because of the varieties of cultural life in which it finds itself, speaking languages, engaging in conversations in labor union, in factory, in offices of management, dealing with the problems of life not because of any special virtue but simply because the Gospel is constantly moving, constantly challenging.

So Luther could be excommunicated from the church of his day and yet know that he was still a member of the Church! He could dare to burn the Papal Edict and believe that he was still in the communion of saints. It is this kind of understanding that could be superbly translated into twentieth-century church life, setting a believer free from the other-directed conformity and the easy iconoclasm of the "God is dead," "parish is dead" lament. Old semantic patterns may not communicate, old packages may be dull, old forms may be dead, but the Church is alive in new forms, new ways and in new understanding. Luther declared: "What the church says is not the Word of God, but the Word of God says what the Church will be. The Church does not make the word but is made by the Word." [1]

That round-robin letter which we know as Ephesians bore the description of the church as a building fitly framed together, but growing. There was a dynamic about the form, a change about the architecture, a new crisis in each age. Yet the substance was there as the center of the crisis.

Christian Community • Where there are those who believe in books, there is a library. Where there are those who believe in sports, there is a team. Where there are those who believe in health and welfare, there are hospitals and socially-concerned institutions. Where the Gospel is preached, the community of believers comes into existence —there is the Church. Its total organization is simply in order that this Gospel be rightly preached and shared in the multitudes of ways in which the people of God find themselves today. God is the ruler over this Church.

Dr. E. Clifford Nelson eloquently witnessed to the Lutheran World Federation in Helsinki, "The church is persons, men and women, called to be the people of God by the Word, and acting as the people of God by serving the Word. Whether the people of God assemble as congregations or as Synods in specific localities—they are ekklesia, for the one Christ is present whole and undivided in every assembly of believers who are served by and who serve the Word and Sacraments."[2]

If we are to explore space and the far-reaches of the universe, then the believer is concerned that the same worth of man and the dignity of the human soul and the redemption of the love of God be known in and through those explorations. In that sense, the Gospel of Christ moves in and through human beings. The church is in trouble when it tries to ignore this dynamic witness. Jesus spoke plainly of the salt losing its worth and the light being taken from the candlestick. History is replete with illustrations.

Luther felt this strongly. He thought of the church of that time as taking into itself the total authority for the Word of God. If any human organization tried to supplant this kingdom of God, and if their leaders attempted to substitute their own will for the will of God, then (as now), that church was in error. Just joining a church or being a pastor or leader is not enough. It is more than that. It was the faith of the believer. He could be a pastor, and be lost. He could be a leader, and have no power. He could live in the company of Christians, and not be a

Christian. A person could subsidize that which he would not imitate. This was the dangerous and heretical Gospel of the Reformation. It was enough to cause excommunication and the burning of "heretics" in that age. If this doesn't seem dangerous in our time, it may be that we have become too secularized to be aware.

If it is dangerous to think of leadership or a clerical authority taking unto itself this claim to the Gospel, it is as important that the individual not think of himself as the final authority. The claiming of a personal opinion as the cloak for the will of God becomes the opposite danger. So Protestantism has had to fight against this dual danger of a clericalism on one side and of a false personalizing of the Gospel on the other.

In our own time there has been ample witness to the continuing need for the boldness of this Gospel. The Lutheran Church in Germany that did not witness alertly enough concerning the evils of the Nazis, still produced such amazing prophets as Dietrich Bonhoefer and the Confessional Church. The Church in America which may seem to be out of touch with life in many instances still produces a leadership in moral and social questions which enables men to sense that there is a nerve-center which has been overlooked. When the Church is concerned about its stance in public events, it becomes self-conscious and vulnerable; when it is concerned that there must be a Christian witness in circulation, then it possesses the power of that Gospel. When God calls a man, he must be prepared to die; so with the priesthood of believers, the Church.

Church Polity · The church is not just an association of persons, no matter how laudable their intentions. *The Church is the body of Christ.* This Evangelical Church, sustained by Gospel and the experience of those who had known this Gospel: saints, apostles, prophets, martyrs, and reformers, has witnessed across the centuries. When Luther engaged in his stalwart work, it was not to organize a new church, but to purify and strengthen the existing church. In the sixteenth century there was no other road to travel and remain true to this Gospel. In our own day, Christians are not called to maintain ancient divisions; they are called to explore the Christian witness, its experience, its tradition, its vocation in today's world—to purify and strengthen the witness of Christ. The truth of God is not in the hands of the church; the truth *about* God and this witness concerning His impact upon life *is* in the hands of the church.

Lutherans do not think of the church as having been started in the sixteenth century by a man in contrast to the church founded by Christ. They believe they are a part of the holy catholic church stretching through the centuries. Martin Luther was one of the leaders who played an important role in this witness of the church, but the history of Lutheranism begins in the life of Christ, not in Martin Luther. The Apostles' and Nicene Creeds, the prayers and hymns of the early church, the witness of saints and teachers are all reflected in the life and experience of Lutheranism. The Reformation caused a break in the organizational unity; it does not expel but rather desires to restore the primary meaning of the faith and life of Christendom.

Lutheranism finds itself understanding the relationship of the Church and the churches just as it understands the meaning of the congregation and the individual Christian. Its center of authority is in the justification of the believer, *sole fide, sola Scriptura*. To function, these Christians are bound together as parts of a body, to use Paul's paraphrase. Thus the pastor, schooled, educated, trained in a theological seminary and properly examined and ordained by the association of these churches, becomes a leader. Spiritually he is one of the congregation. His call comes from the congregation, authorized by the association of congregations, usually called the Synod. These Synods give to their officers certain duties which cannot be performed by any single congregation alone. Thus the problems of education, the preparation of educational materials, social and moral decisions, the establishment of new congregations, the work of world missions, and the care of the infirm, elderly and the helpless becomes the work of the congregation of congregations. This central congregation is not just a federation or cooperative unit. It has form, substance and body; yet its power is derived from the congregations.

All of the boards, agencies and commissions of the congregation, the local Synod and the national Church have men and women of the parishes who give time and energy coupled with their experience, their talent and their faith in expressing this faith in the multiplicity of activities of this international fellowship.

In the United States and Canada, the leaders of these Synods are known as Presidents elected in a democratic assembly of the delegates from congregations. In Europe they are usually known as Bishops. The chief difference is simply that in the transferral of the church into the Western world, at the time of the surge of democratic methods, it seemed wise not to give life tenure to leaders. You can have an ex-President but not an ex-Bishop. Now that the Lutheran World Federation binds together the 75 million Lutherans of the world in a cooperative assembly, there is an increasing understanding of the term and office of the Bishop with numbers of Americans desiring the use of this term in the United States.

The Church and the Churches • To be a Lutheran is not to be a separatist. It is to belong to a church which is bound together by a confessional consciousness and a desire that there be unity of faith between all Christians. It is this search for the meaning of the Gospel in contemporary life which has taken great sections of the Lutheran communion into the councils of and leadership of the World Council of Churches and the bold new cooperative ventures of Christendom. Most Lutherans have felt that the spirit of the heroic Martin Luther's "Here I stand" cannot be maintained in individualist or singular purpose but rather in terms of the common witness of all Christians who confess Christ as divine Lord and thus have grounds for common action. There are Lutherans who have felt that they have jeopardized their calling to preserve a "pure doctrine" or orthodox Lutheran theology by involvement in ecumenical dialogue. Most Lutherans believe that in the competition of present ideologies there is a clear call to discover those things that unite all Christians, while understanding these differences in faith and practice which might keep from a complete organizational merger. There are others who strongly feel that this places the Lutheran, who is concerned with his Christian witness, in a compromising situation.

On one thing all are agreed. On all sides there is a renewal of the exploration of the basic Christian doctrines that bind men together. Not even the *Augsburg Confession* can become a static slogan. Whether it be in the action or reaction created by ecumenism, or by the struggle against communism or competing religious philosophies in various places of the world, there is a theological and doctrinal discussion that the churches may know better what unites and what divides them.

To believe in and pray for the unity of the church is to dedicate one's self to the ideal, and to meet one's brothers in every faith with respect and understanding. This is the good in the new mood. Grateful as Lutherans are for this open window which has allowed so many breezes to blow through, it is not unmannerly for the Lutheran to ask of others that which he must ask of himself, that we approach our problems as equals, "as God calls, gathers and enlightens the whole Christian family on earth."

For instance, recent statements by the Roman Catholic hierarchy concerning mixed marriages are headlined as important relaxations. When this change only means that a Protestant minister can be present in vestments, can congratulate the young couple, and can acquiesce to a promise that the children be reared in the Roman Catholic faith, this hardly seems to be a satisfactory relaxation.

Ecumenism is not closing one's eyes. It is recognizing what we are, and why we are what we are, and then with grateful optimism and respectful honesty working to bridge the gaps. It is a time to be honestly self-critical, honestly humble, honestly receptive, and honestly desirous of a reunited organization which presents the fact of the Church to mankind.

K. E. Skydsgaard has written that Roman Catholicism and Lutheranism must not only bear their separation but must never accept it as normal or matter-of-fact. "It is actually screamingly not normal. The 'no' which is erected here as a wall between them must early and late be a cause for repentance and a renewed eagerness to seek their common 'yes': the confession of the living Lord and his presence in the worship of the church. In that worship the decisive thing can never be what we do or accomplish but what Christ speaks and works. In the midst of the 'no,' there is a 'yes.'" [3]

The Expression of the Church • The idea of a spiritual community expresses itself in the congregational existence of the church, a form or body which is best known to the believer. So church becomes congregation and believer becomes member and faith becomes practice.

In Roman Catholicism all powers are derived through the Vicar of Christ, as the Pope is known, and so through the hierarchy to the local member. In Lutheranism the process is reversed. Nothing could stand between the individual and his Lord. This included the organization of the church.

The local congregation may be a company of believers in an immediate neighborhood or a metropolitan congregation in the neighborhood of the metropolis. It will be a parish—a company of people who share a spiritual relationship. It is not an aggregation but a congregation. It is not an assembly but a community. It is not an audience but a family. It has form and shape but it is not a rigid structure. Its form is reformable. The local congregation becomes the rootage, growing not as a single isolated plant, but as a harvest, belonging to the whole as the whole belongs to the single plant.

Its system of government varies but it is generally governed by a Church Council of which a layman may be the President. The Pastor, Seminary-trained and Synod-ordained, is called by the congregation to be its leader in spiritual and temporal affairs. Martin Marty has called the government of the Lutheran Church "Presbygational." That is, it has a group of elders and/or Deacons and is autonomous. Yet it exists as a member of the territorial Synod and it gives many of its rights and privileges to this larger company of congregations. These Synods are bound into a national or international church.

The minister of the congregation is usually called "Pastor." A traditional term referring to Shepherd, it nonetheless perfectly expresses the ideal of this relationship. The pastor is not just a spiritual or congregational director; he is the counselor and leader, called to publicly express the faith and life of these people in the world; to share this deeply with all those who witness, not only with those associated with the congregation. It is an impossible ideal with its tension known by pastor and people alike in its inner responsibilities and its external possibilities.

The concept of pastor is a respected and honored one within the congregation, although the office has been subjected to all of the re-evaluations and changes that confront every perplexed profession. It is not always as certain that its exercise is one which Gregory called "the art of arts." The problem of maintaining a close pastoral relationship, sharing in the total life of the community, serving as preacher and teacher, subjects the honest man to torments of personal concern. The public and private relationship of the Lutheran pastor still offers an important reason for existence; the true pastor does not have to search for his sense of relationship to needs and possibilities—they pound at his door.

The Lutheran pastor is called by the congregation and this call is approved or ratified by the Synodical office. The length of the pastorate is determined by a number of personal or social situations. In contrast to some churches where there have been frequent changes of pastorate, Lutheran pastors have remained throughout a longer period. One of my own predecessors was an active, creative and imaginative pastor and prophet in the same congregation for 47 years.

In the mobility of our years, this continuity has had increasing value. The frequent changes of membership within the congregation, the swift ebb and flow of the neighborhood and the challenges within the city, require a sense of stability. The pastor who is in the right place and has the opportunity to serve, becomes more than a local congregational director. He is truly the pastor who experiences shepherding far beyond the immediate concerns of his own congregation. In and through his office, he exercises this inherent authority as "man of God" and "ambassador for Christ." In today's urban complex he knows new accents of Jesus' statement that there are sheep outside the fold.

Perhaps the most dramatic tests confronting the pastor of our time are in the inner-city. The diversities of peoples, the gaps of culture, the enormous tensions, the predicaments confronting the silent poor and the wordless affluent, all reveal the need of evangelical witness. No one knows the pat answer or the exact route to travel. We are much like Thomas standing before his Lord asking, "How can we know the way"? To which Jesus replied with cogent understanding to Thomas and to us, "I am the way the truth and the life." To follow that way opens up the exciting possibilities of the pastor-congregation relationship in the contradictions and complexities of our time.

The Lutheran pastor may be—and most generally is—a married man. The home and family of the pastor play an important role in the life of the congregation and in the community. The marriage of Martin Luther and Katherine von Bora marked a symbolic, as well as, deeply personal act. The pastor is a man of the people of God, a man among men, and his family is a family among the families.

The Women of the Church · No story of the Lutheran community can be told without appreciation of the leadership of the women of the church. Not only in its dedicated deaconesses and its many missionaries and not only in the offices of leadership in the local congregation, is the story told. This leadership in the local organizational structure is important. Here in these groups has been an educational dialogue, an information center concerning the faith and life of the church. These women have raised millions of dollars, subsidized all kinds and sorts of programs within the structure of the church and have exerted a continuing witness in the community. Impressive as are the statistics, the most important fact is that women have shared in the life of the community, have witnessed in the counsels of the church, and have participated in the adventure of the Christian witness.

As a matter of fact, within the church, women learned to preside, to develop and to express qualities of leadership and to participate in the total life of the church. Now that is being expressed in a new social and ecumenical witness. They are sharing this vocational concern in the world where faith is the power of endless discovery.

In several of the Scandinavian and European countries women have been accepted into the ministry of the church. For years they have been a part of the Diaconate; they have served as teachers in theological schools and have shared in the developing thought of the church. Now they are recognized in a new relationship. The matter is not yet tested in the United States but each year finds more women students in our theological seminaries.

The Total Ministry · I like the words of Mark Gibbs in *God's Frozen People* when he states, "The essential job of the minister is not to do something for me but to help me to do something for myself: not to pray for me, but to help me pray, not to worship in my name, but to help me offer my worship with the worship of the church. . . . The unique things that the minister does in the name of the Church, such as celebrating the Sacraments, he does with me and other men. In it I have my part to play." [4] This is a contemporary statement of this pastor-laity relationship, an essential of the reformation faith which is of renewed importance now.

Through Synod (the territorial organizations of churches) and the national body—its board and agencies, the faith of these people is expressed in activities that range from worship to social action, from parish education to world missions, from collecting the gifts of the faithful to the spending of millions in national and world programs, from evangelization of the local neighborhood to concern for the evangelism in press, radio and television, from the especially provincial concerns of the parish to the ecumenical and worldwide concerns which are also a part of the parish. The congregation and the Synod are thus not rivals but part and parcel of the same body and this same pastoral relationship must be known. This is the ideal to which the Lutheran congregation aspires and wherever it falls down in this expression, it defeats that which itself confesses.

The Larger Fellowship · The six purposes of the Lutheran World Federation express the national yearning of this community:

1) To bear united witness before the world to the Gospel of Jesus Christ as the power of God for salvation;
2) To cultivate unity of faith and confession among the Lutheran churches of the world;
3) To promote fellowship and cooperation in study among Lutherans;
4) To foster Lutheran participation in Ecumenical movements;
5) To develop a united Lutheran approach to responsibilities in Missions and Education;
6) To support Lutheran groups in view of spiritual or material aid.

To be a member of the local parish is to share in that search.

Missions and Mission • At first the Reformation was local, dealing with the immediate situations. The names of the local communities are represented in the signatories of the Augsburg Confession. This event and experience rippled out in wave after wave of impact so that Lutheranism is truly an international community. Later this same urgency that sent men to the colonial America, sent men and women to every sector of the planet. To believe is to be committed to mission!

The church that is a household cannot be contained in a country, an economic or cultural class, or in a language. The story of the witness of Christian missionaries is not only an evidence of global concern but of the new and creative ways in which the faith is shared and the new forms in which it is expressed. Two thousand men and women of the United States and Canada represent the Lutheran churches of these countries as they express this sense of mission in 24 countries of the world. In the international experiences of this century the forms of missions will change: mission remains. This is the Church coming and becoming. This is the Body of Christ, the live voice of the Gospel.

IX

The Heritage of Faith:
The Reformation

Lord, Jesus Christ, thy power
   make known
For thou art Lord of Lords
   alone;
Defend thy Christendom, that
   we
May evermore sing praise to thee.
      —M. Luther

When the historian MacKinnon wrote of the Reformation, he penned a memorable sentence, "The greatest fact of the sixteenth century is that Luther was." In every historical situation some individual becomes the personification of the idea. Virtues are never abstract. Goodness becomes known in a good man, evil in a hateful man. It is still true that "by their fruits ye shall know them." In the days of the Reformation the simmering desires for freedom, the resentments against the abuses in the Church and the antagonism rising against the legacy of the Renaissance Papacy became vocal in the experience, the struggle and the expression of faith in a genius-leader, Martin Luther.

Born in 1483, he came into life at a time when unrelated and dynamic forces were at work. The development of the printing press had played a decisive part. Heretics could be burned at the stake but the printing of pamphlets enabled men to outflank such tyranny. New worlds were being discovered and novel ideas concerning the universe were evolving. The world of that time was coming apart. In such an age Luther, the son of a miner in Eisleben, studied to become a lawyer. "He was a true son of the Church. His spiritual life had been enkindled and nurtured from the Church's ministrations of word and sacrament. Devout parents had trained him from childhood in the fear of God. The daily worship to which he was accustomed, long before he found the Bible at Erfurt, familiarized him with some truth for the faith of his heart to grasp. Luther is to be regarded not as the founder of a new church or as the leader of a school of church life and thought so much as the representative and heir of all that was noblest and best in medieval Christianity; and as the pioneer of a new order of things only insofar as he fearlessly carried to their conclusions the promises that others were either unable or unwilling to apply." [1]

Luther the lawyer, through a series of dramatic events, became Luther the theologian and so a priest of the church in the Augustinian order. Trained in the theology expounded by St. Augustine, he discovered truths which were to burn throughout the remainder of his days. Preparing a lecture on the Psalms he came across such words as Psalm 71:2, "Deliver me in thy righteousness." To Luther this was no simple academic matter; this was the description of his own life. He had watched men contributing money for indulgences. He had been repelled by a Tetzel with his drums pounding and his call for florins for St. Peter's in Rome: "As soon as the coin in the coffer rings, the soul from purgatory springs."

Dietrich Bonhoeffer discovered the inspiration for his own dramatic thrust into the turmoil of his own time by remembering the life of Luther. "When the Reformation came, the providence of God raised Martin Luther to restore the gospel of pure, costly grace. Luther passed through the cloister; he was a monk, and all this was part of the divine plan. Luther had left all to follow Christ on the path of absolute obedience. He had renounced the world to live the Christian life . . . But God shattered his hopes. He showed him through the Scripture that the following of Christ is not the achievement of or merit of a select few, but the divine command to all Christians without distinction . . . Luther's return from the cloister to the world was the worst blow the world had suffered since the days of early Christianity. The renunciation he made when he became a monk was child's play compared with that which he had to make when he returned to the world. Now came the frontal assault. The only way to follow Jesus was by living in the world." [2]

Luther had known this struggle in his own life. He found an answer to his struggle and to the prayer of the Psalmist in the letter to the Romans: "For therein is the righteousness of God, revealed from faith unto faith; as it is written, the just shall live by faith." So the personal struggle became the active exploration which led this sturdy monk to nail 95 theses to the door of the Castle Church in Wittenberg in 1517. To circulate this document at this strategic point was a bold protest.[3] These 95 statements contained such affirmations as:

1. Our Lord and Master Jesus Christ, when he said "Repent," willed that the whole life of the believer should be repentance.
8. The penitential canons are imposed only on the living and, according to them, nothing should be imposed on the dying.
43. Christians are to be taught that giving to the poor or lending to the needy is better than to buy indulgences.
82. Why does not the pope empty purgatory for the sake of holy love and the dire needs of the souls instead of for the sake of miserable money with which to build a church?

This was a daring act. Yet it was not in the act itself, but in the content of the deed that the drama erupted.

It was customary for an academic leader to present theses which would be debated by his fellow scholars. This was what Luther intended at the moment. The event became the challenge to the authority of the church and to the expressions of this authority in the sale of indulgences, in the denial of a personal faith, and in the extreme demand for all authority of mind and conscience within the boundaries of the church itself. To this he protested and the name which was spit at him was "Protestant." It became an honorable term much as the name "Christian" has been hallowed after those early days in Antioch, when it was a mark of derision.

If this does not seem as startling in our time, it must be recognized as an assault against the established church in the sixteenth century, a heritage which ought never to be taken for granted. It is the beginning of our educational development. It is a remarkable struggle for religious freedom. It is at the heart of much of that which is involved in the struggle of the twentieth century. At its center was "solus Christus: Christ alone; sola gratia: by grace alone; sola fide: by faith alone." Everything that flowered from this fact should have issued in the strengthened, united Christian fellowship. Instead it erupted into a divisiveness which startled his generation and challenges our own. In the twentieth century it could blossom into a renewed unity. The "tragic necessity" of the sixteenth century is relevant to the development of a renewing unity and witness in the twentieth century.

That which Luther expressed had been felt by others— he became spokesman and leader. Within a short time great scholars such as Melanchthon were at his side, political leaders for noble or selfish ends were supporting his cause, ambitious iconoclasts were attempting to exploit his daring and rigid opponents were unbelievingly trying to call off the fight by outmoded methods.

The movement which we note in its beginning in 1517 grew until 1530 when a Diet or ecclesiastical assembly was held in Augsburg to state the theological dimensions of this faith. *The Augsburg Confession* is today the accepted document of the Lutheran Church everywhere and becomes the confessional platform upon which 75 million Lutherans stand, even when they express the tenets of this document in diverse ways. The protest grew into a movement which found form and structure.

This is the dilemma of Protestantism. It is its heritage that it is a protest but it cannot remain so. It became involved in the faith that God's power is constantly present, always and constantly reforming, and is false to its heritage if it freezes or attempts to stultify this power in unchanging forms. The Lutheran way of life is an understanding of this reverence concerning the Word of God as brought through Word and Sacraments, and so moving with prophetic and evangelical ardor in the whole of today's life. To call oneself Lutheran is to know this dynamic urgency and this search for a new unity.

An illustration of the paradox is simply stated in Luther's sermon concerning "service." "The word 'service' related to the word 'servant' has been much abused. We talk about the church Service and we have reference to the ringing of bells in the church of wood or stone, to the liturgy, the gold and silk of jewels in the vestments, the Chalice, the monstrance, the organ and images, processions and cloisters, and above all, the babbling and saying of rosaries. This is called the church service." In another way *this* is our dilemma. The modern idiom of worship dare not become a contemporary substitute for these ancient forms.

Luther had been trained in the universities, having achieved Bachelor and Masters degrees in the Arts, and then had majored in law, before entering into rigorous theological studies. It was in this atmosphere of the university and in the knowledge of the related areas of learning, not just as an isolated theologian, that he came to his position of protest against the sale of indulgences and began his titanic struggle with the church of his day.

As a result of his disciplines and as an expression of his own particular nature he wrote, preached, spoke and published. Tracts, essays, introductions to Biblical books and hymns erupted from his study. Of the 208 books published in all of Germany in 1520, 133 of them were written by Luther. His translation of the Scriptures from Latin, Greek and Hebrew into the German language gave a semantic unity to the nation as well as a religious heritage. His daring to stand against any of the authorities of church or state made him the dominant figure of his century. And, as Durant has stated, "Luther proclaimed that no man could be saved unless he renounced the rule of the papacy. The monk had excommunicated the Pope." [4]

In the liturgy and hymnody Luther gave the church a catholicity of worship in the vernacular. More important to the worshipper in the pew is the liturgy, but to the household is the statement of the Catechism. In the brief document of the Catechism he set forth questions and answers concerning the *Ten Commandments,* the *Apostles Creed,* the *Lord's Prayer, Baptism* and the *Lord's Supper,* plus family prayers. These became the spinal column of the teaching content of the Lutheran preparing for church membership into our own time. He took the abstractions of the theological struggle and placed them in a simple, teaching procedure for the family and the parish.

Concerning the teaching functions of the Church, Luther insisted that such questions as these must be dealt with. What is the Law? What is the Gospel? What is sin? What is grace? What is true repentance? How true confession is made? What is faith? What is forgiveness of sins? What is Christian liberty? What is free will? What is hope? What is love? What is the Cross? What is Baptism? Deep at the center is the agony of understanding the meaning of self and the grace of God. This tension of the deep inadequacy of man to pull himself up by his own bootstraps on the one hand or, on the other hand, to appease God by rites, ceremonies, deeds, gifts or acts left man in the horror of his sin. He could ignore this by pretending that life is simply an interval to be made as beautiful as possible. He could turn it over to an institution to handle, to make its decrees and formulae, and thus to lose the meaning of the individual in the security of the enveloping organization, or he could begin to understand the sanctity of the individual with its risks as well as its freedom. If this is true, and if there is a Word of God which is known in and through the Scriptures which takes precedence over tradition, then God's gifts to man must be received, understood and used.

Luther spoke on all manner of public issues and, as a result, was involved in debates which caused him to be misquoted in our own century. He was a child of the sixteenth century. He was no saint but a very human human being. He knew this. He was tortured by the thoughts of his own guilt. He struggled with sin. He knew the depths of that agony and could not be won off by scholastic arguments, appeased by pious devotions or threatened by ecclesiastical condemnations. He was a man, but he was God's man!

In 1521, Charles V of the Holy Roman Empire came to Germany and called a Diet or conference in the city of Worms. These princes and representatives of the state met with Luther and he was confronted with these books and essays which he had written. In the *Liberty of the Christian Man* he had dealt with the freedom from slavery; therefore, the freedom for service of the Christian. In his

Letter to the Christian Nobility he had attacked the unnatural separation between the priest and the layman. In the "Babylonian Captivity of the Church" he had presented the doctrine of the real presence in the Lord's Supper as opposed to the Roman teaching of transubstantiation.

These and others of his writings he was now asked to disown. He was a courageous man but he knew the dire consequences politically and socially of excommunication, as well as the spiritual tension. Nonetheless, after a soul-struggle he was able to say, "Since then Your Majesty and your lordships desire a simple reply, I will answer without horns and without teeth. Unless I am convicted by Scripture and plain reason—I do not accept the authority of popes and councils, for they have contradicted each other —my conscience is captive to the Word of God. I cannot and will not recant anything, for to go against conscience is neither right nor safe. God help me. Amen." He had burned the Bull of excommunication; now his life was in jeopardy.

In the midst of his struggles he also maintained a personal life. He married Katherine von Bora and his family life with his children became a kind of model for familyhood throughout the centuries. His pastoral concern was expressed constantly and consistently. His dealings with the problems of church and state, war and peace, peasants and noblemen embroiled him in controversies. He was alive to social issues, expressing his faith in the midst of the tensions of his own day. Faith was a living-ness!

We live in a time when we would like to come up with easy answers, wanting a kind of moral, doctrinal and ethical machine which, by pressing the appropriate button, produces the answer. The Lutheran finds himself with neither Vatican Council nor authoritative voice within his group. He has the obligation of discovering this voice as it comes from the authority of the Scriptures within the church, the priesthood of believers. It is this communion of saints which imposes new and challenging obligations in a time when it would be easier to allow a leader to speak. It is just here that contemporary Christians renew this need to develop a creative dialogue. The Christian has no easy answers, but he does have a dynamic, confident spirit.

Paul Tillich once put the matter succinctly. Speaking of the Protestant heritage he wrote, "The Protestant principle overcomes the gap between the sacred and the secular spheres, between priesthood and laity. Protestantism demands a radical laicism. There are in Protestantism only laymen; the minister is a layman with a special function within the congregation; and, in addition to possessing certain personal requisites, he is qualified for the fulfillment of his function by carefully regulated professional training. He is a non-layman solely by virtue of his training." [5] To understand this it is necessary to understand this relation of pastor and people. Protestant laymen are to challenge any conscious or unconscious attempt of ministers or theologians (non-laymen) to set up a religious sphere as separate from his "secular" life or "secular" work. He is to tear down this boundary.

The heritage of dialogue created the ferment that produced the catechism, translated Scriptures, propelled educational and missionary efforts. When the Church is at its best, it is not fettered by tradition, by state or by any of its own shackles. It is emerging from sheer stagnation into the open air of intellectual discussion with the world.

This was the Christian heritage of the first centuries of its existence. Jesus dealt gratefully with the whole heritage of his past. He took it as God's word. "I have come not to destroy but to fulfill." In this spirit he enlarged the dimensions of law and broke through the burden of fear with the shared grace of God; it took him to a cross—it was here that men spoke of "the atoning love of God" not as magic but as dynamic forgiveness. This is at the very heartbeat of the Lutheran's understanding of life.

This brought Luther into all areas of life and he wrote with such zest and bluntness that we are offended in some of our more polite situations of the present. The contemporary Lutheran cannot enshrine Luther nor ignore him. He understands him as a religious genius, one of God's most useful and influential witnesses. He was a faithful man through whom flowed a liberating spirit. The church that stands against Mariolatry does not engage in a "Reformer-olatry."

Luther did not come into this alone. He was at the apex of a smoldering movement which had begun centuries before, which found its emphasis in statements by such saints as Augustine and in such protests as Hus and Savonarola. He was also helped by intellectual and religious companions who shared in the prodigious writing that was produced. He was helped—and often burdened—by the political assistance of princes and governments who welcomed the Reformation for non-religious reasons. The religious fervor that moved these men may produce the same dilemma in modern Christianity. For, if we are the communion of saints, we must stand not only against tyrants as did so many thousands during World War II but over the total prophetic ministry of those who call themselves Christian.

It is the burden of Lutheranism that it has been charged with divisiveness. In the sense that it protested and brought into the open the long history of religious debate, this is a correct charge. Yet Luther believed, as Jaroslav Pelikan states it succinctly, "the church had been Christian and Catholic before the Papacy; therefore, it could be both Christian and Catholic without the Papacy. In the name of such Christian catholicity the reformers were willing to challenge Rome." [6]

In another context Dr. Pelikan emphasizes the fact that "it is the genius of Luther's Reformation that in it both Catholic substance and Protestant principle came to voice. In his treatment of the dogmatic, conciliar and liturgical tradition of Catholic Christianity Luther proved to be an obedient rebel—or, to use terms coined in another context, an orthodox heretic, a respectable agitator, an intellectual Philistine, a conservative revolutionary." [7]

With all of the stormy events peppering his life, it is astonishing to sense the freedom of action and zest for living that he was able to express. He was under the ban of the church and the empire, yet he was able to move with a quick courage and unalloyed enthusiasm. His followers had protested vigorously, and now they were known as "Protestants." Later there was this significant company which would be known as "Lutheran." For Luther himself there was only the desire that he be a child and pupil of salvation in Christ and that he maintained until death came to him in his 62nd year in 1546.

At the risk of oversimplification, this Protestant heritage states:

1. Faith in the God we know through Jesus Christ as the Lord and Saviour of all.

2. Belief that the Word of God is known through the Scriptures in a unique way, and therefore to be cherished and understood.

3. The grace of God is mediated through the life of Christ, and man can neither understand himself nor God until he understands this love through Christ.

4. Man's sin is overcome by this grace of God and not through his own efforts. Therefore, we are justified by this faith alone and bound into the priesthood of believers.

5. The credal confessions of the church become the co-

hesive unit which binds Christians together but do not limit their minds or spirits.

6. Since man is responsibly free, he has the responsibility of understanding, of teaching, of sharing, of witnessing in the total area of life.

7. Since there is no division between the sacred and the secular, all art and culture can express this power of God. Therefore, anything that can be so understood is welcome, not because of any intrinsic worth in itself but because it can develop into a "belief-ful realism."

8. Faith begins in worship, continues in the life of the church, is shared in educational and cultural witness, and appeals to the committed allegiance of all persons.

Luther looked through the paradox of his day and discovered the reality of God. This heritage is not enriched by rehearsing the debates of the sixteenth century. The problem today is not in the tensions between Protestants and Catholics but rather in the tensions between Christianity and the competing ideologies. Today's world has inherited the meaning of the individual, has known the rivalries of great faiths, and once more sees the movement toward reunion. The heritage of the Reformation is in entering the dialogue of the twentieth century with the sense of Luther's urgency that the truth might be known. He charged into the issues of his day, dealing with every problem and personality. Lutheranism at its best brings this same sense of holy confidence into the dialogue and the debates of the present, willing that ancient forms may die in order that the truth expressed through those forms be known. The future of the dialogue is as challenging and as unpredictable as the dialogue of the sixteenth century.

A recent Roman Catholic appraisal of Lutheranism in this sense states:

The Lutheran religious attitude, rich in itself and deeply rooted, concentrates on the person, work, and all embracing grace of Jesus Christ. Consciousness of the Redeemer's sanctifying activity here and now in every sincere believer has been carefully preserved as Luther's heritage. It finds expression in, among other things, the Lutheran's conviction of the Lord's real presence in the eucharist, in the specific devoutness of their numerous hymns and in their domestic worship. What St. Clement Hofbauer said in 1816 about the German Reformation is still typical of the Lutherans: "The Reformation came about because the Germans felt and still feel, the need for piety; the Reformation spread and was maintained, not by heretics and philosophers, but by people who really wanted a religion that appealed to the heart." Finally, there arose in most Lutheran churches a movement toward deep reflection on, and more intense practice of, a sacramental and liturgical life. In this they consciously seek closer contact with the old, not yet divided Church.[8]

In a time when our world seems to be coming apart, we remember with gratitude this man of God who became a channel for the confident grace of God to move into the situation of the sixteenth century, certain that God was speaking even when the old world was going to pieces. We can use that quality of faith in the twentieth century!

Notable Dates in the Life of Martin Luther

1483 Martin Luther born at Eisleben on November 10.

1501–1505 Luther achieves University degrees in arts and later trains as a lawyer.

1505–1507 Decides to enter monastery, becomes an Augustinian monk and is ordained as a priest.

1517 On October 31 Luther nails the document "Ninety-Five Theses" on the door of Castle Church at Wittenberg, protesting the sale of indulgences.

1518–1520 Enormous amount of writing and preaching of sermons, such as:
"Address to the Christian Nobles"
"The Babylonian Captivity of the Church"
"Of the Freedom of the Christian Man"
Pope Leo X issues Papal bull threatening excommunication and Luther burns the document in public.

1521 Diet of Worms where Luther refuses to retract his writings, stating, "Here I stand, I can do no other."

1524 First sections of Old Testament translation into German published.

1525 Luther marries Katherine von Bora.

1529 Catechism published.

1530 Writing of the Augsburg Confessions, the great confessional document which still remains basic to the Lutheran Church.

1534 Completion of Luther's translation of the Bible resulting in the first complete edition of the German Bible.

1534–1546 Many disputes and developments in the development of the Protestant community. Luther's extensive religious writings, hymns, sermons beginning to be published and become the strengthening of the church.

1546 Luther has heart attack at Eisleben and dies at the age of 62, buried at Wittenberg.

X

The American Translation:
The Lutheran Church in America

> O Comforter of priceless worth
> Send peace and unity on earth;
> Support us in our final strife,
> And lead us out of death to life.
> —*M. Luther*

Across the wall in East Zone Germany there is a Lutheran church bearing two bronze tablets, memorializing Johan Cruger and Paul Gerhardt. These two indomitable souls shared a singing faith throughout the Thirty Years War. At a time of crisis, they could preach and sing. Wrote Gerhardt:

> Put thou thy trust in God,
> In duty's path go on;
> Walk in His strength with faith and hope,
> So shall thy work be done.[1]

It was a time that men acted on such faith. In 1638 Lutherans from the Netherlands had established churches in New Amsterdam and by 1649 in Albany. John Gutwasser came to New Amsterdam as the first Lutheran pastor in 1657. In Delaware the Swedish Lutherans had established a congregation and Germans were settling in what is now Philadelphia. Palatine Lutherans settled in Pennsylvania and Salzburg Lutherans in Georgia. In 1703 Julius

Falckner, America's first native Lutheran pastor, was ordained. In 1734 the German Salzburgers came to Georgia and Lutheran churches were established.

By the eighteenth century there were these pockets of Lutheranism, a shortage of pastors, frequent breakdowns of communication between the "old country" and the "new." Hardships in the colonial settlements—all added to heartaches and difficulties. It remained for a stalwart German to take the 102-day-journey from Germany to Philadelphia. Thus began the 45-year career of Henry Melchior Muhlenberg, one of the most illustrious of the pioneer churchmen in America. This German Lutheran fit the American spirit. He came with a spirit of pietism and warmth and this, with his amazing energy and talent, stamped him as a natural leader. He traveled throughout the eastern seaboard with *Ecclesia Plantanda* (The Church must be planted) as his sole motto. His travels ranged far and wide and he was known from Nova Scotia to Georgia. As Dr. J. I. Neve described him, "He possessed in an extraordinary degree the grace of finding favor with men." Muhlenberg gave the first Lutheran Order of Services to colonial America.[2]

A historian, Dr. Theodore Bachman, has typified his contributions as:

(1) the first permanent Lutheran Synod, founded in 1748 and now known as the Eastern Pennsylvania Synod;

(2) the introduction of a common liturgy based on a composite of German orders;

(3) the creation of a representative congregational government, complete with constitution that became a model for the future;

(4) the training of men for the pastoral ministry;

(5) a strong emphasis on education and the recruiting of teachers;

(6) a faithful rendering of pastoral care;

(7) the cultivation of stewardship through the voluntary support of pastors, plus the building of churches and schools.

Remembering that this was in a time when a man rode horseback, fording streams and enduring the hardships of colonial America, his accomplishments become further enhanced. He and his wife, Mary Weiser, brought 11 children into the world and one of his sons achieved fame as a leader in the Revolutionary War. It was this son who preached a sermon which closed with the heroic statement, "There is a time to pray and a time to fight, and this is the time to fight." He threw off his robe revealing his regimental uniform. The first speaker of the House of Representatives was also a Muhlenberg.

By the time of the elder Muhlenberg's death in 1787 there were 120,000 Germans in Pennsylvania, people who brought with them their language, their culture, and their religious practices. Yet they now found themselves cut off from their homeland and their church life grew along with their national life.

These Lutherans were independent and freedom-loving, even to the point of divisiveness. The great names of Samuel Schmucker, Charles Philip Krauth, Ferdinand Walther and others indicate stalwart believers and leaders who made great independent contributions to the American scene. They began to establish colleges and seminaries. They led whole communities into new areas. Grabau and his followers rooted themselves in Buffalo in 1839 while Walther moved with his followers into Missouri in 1841. Likewise Norwegians, Swedes, Danes, Finns, and Icelandic peoples joined the precessional that streamed from Europe. Names such as Eielsen, Preus, Esbjorn, Nikander joined the Germanic names as new residents from Scandinavian countries swarmed into the midwest and out through the western sections of the nation.

Not all of these new settlers were eager to become associated with the church. In fact only a small percentage actually became affiliated with early American Lutheranism. Some of them insisted on following old world language and cultural patterns so there were German Lutherans, Swedish Lutherans, Norwegian Lutherans and Finnish Lutherans.

The divisions were not only in language and background. These strong-willed people who could gather a hundred followers to join them in migrating to a new world also had a toughness concerning their faith. Various synodical groupings were established and soon the Buffalo Synod, the Iowa Synod, the Joint Synod of Ohio, and the Missouri Synod were much more than groupings within a state. They filtered through the nation and in the twentieth century these ancient groupings are now involved in the hopeful rediscovery of their common faith. As a result of these factors, Lutheranism in early American life was confessionally conservative, sometimes culturally isolationist, but vigorously aggressive and loyal. In the mid-twentieth century some of these virtues are now expressing themselves in a confessional ecumenism led by the grandsons of these men of faith.

The problem of these early pioneers was that they were necessarily bound by cultural ties which are not effective in the lives of their descendants. Sometimes their very Christian faith was hindered in communication by their cultural bonds. Rolvaag, the author who came from just such a Norwegian background, discusses the agony in his book, *Peder Victorious*. He tells of the difficulty encountered with the teen-age son who wants to use the English language. His angry father forbids this in the household and as the youngster stands at his bedroom window where he has been banished, he watches the rain splashing against the panes. He almost laughs as he says, "Even God weeps tonight." It is this conflict in culture which was often identified with a kind of religious antagonism that many times drove sincere Lutherans into a kind of fallout shelter in which they tried to protect themselves from the world, the flesh and the Devil. Sometimes they were only gathering their cultural ties instead of exploring their deep theological rootage or their confessional heritage. The interpretation of that which has happened in America—and which is not unique with the Lutheran experience—is indicative of this problem.

In various cities there has been the confusing spectacle of three Lutheran churches on opposite corners; a caricature which modern man cannot tolerate. There are usually sound historical reasons. In the nineteenth century the struggle between the conservative and liberal wings of the church brought divisions which perpetuated themselves in congregations. The immediate issue has long since passed but the institutions remained. Now it becomes difficult to overcome the resistance to change and to form the institutions which are worthy channels of the Gospel in this century. History is replete with the perpetuation of the forms of division which have lingered long after the reasons for or even the knowledge of the situation has vanished. Fortunately, the old enmities are going and there remains only the need to recover the urgency that overcomes the nostalgia for "dear old First Church."

Nineteenth-century Lutheranism is the story of an evolving at-homeness in the new experience of America. What were scattered congregations gradually found themselves in strong groupings known as Synods. The General Synod, which carried the tradition of leaders like Schmucker and others in the East was founded in 1820. The General Council was a conservative protest; the Augustana Synod was the strong Swedish group; The Synodical Conference founded in 1871 (largely dominated by the Lutheran Church-Missouri Synod), provided another strong, alert, conservative church.

This became the pattern with a variety of smaller synodical groupings embracing various conservative or more liberal persuasions. Perhaps the greatest shock to this situation came with the First World War. Its anti-German wave caused much second thinking on the part of those who had accepted a situation without having analyzed it. Now, many Lutherans did some rigorous soul-searching.

Another factor had come to America, namely the emerging mobility whereby the tightly knit ethnic groups were now dispersed and divided. The old provincialism became shattered and loyalties were tested. As their grandparents took an old world culture with them, these third- and fourth-generation Americans now moved into the full stream of a vigorous surge of national energy. Congregations were established, colleges were founded and a whole series of social institutions for children and for the elderly came into existence.

The signs of a movement in another direction came into emphasis in 1917 with the formation of the United Lutheran Church in America. The American Lutheran Church then emerged along with the Lutheran Church-Missouri Synod. There were the evidences of a new Lutheran ecumenism. The National Lutheran Council enabled these groups to work together. While the Missouri Synod did not become a member of this group, it cooperated in many of its ventures. In 1964 the new possibilities for a true federation of Lutheran activities came into being with the plan to form a Lutheran Council of the United States of America which comes into reality in 1967. The work of this cooperative Lutheranism in relief programs around the world, in meeting the challenge of military bases and threats of war, in social concern in the care of the needy, mentally disturbed and the aging is a striking witness to a dynamic working together that was out ahead of the actual Lutheran organizational agreements. For instance, Lutheran World Relief through the

National Lutheran Council distributed more than a billion pounds of clothing and $44 millions in relief projects since World War II!

Lutherans had turned a new corner in their American history. There was a vague discontent with just praising the past or taking comfort in some pseudo-cultural unity. Life could not be based on language or custom or tradition. The shape of the content needed redescription. Just to sing A *Mighty Fortress Is Our God* was not enough. Lutherans became a part of the exciting struggle and, indeed, shaped the events in many ways which created the possibilities of the struggle. Today American Lutheran leaders such as Franklin Clark Fry, Frederick Schiotz, Conrad Bergendoff, Oliver Harms, Frederick Nolde, Paul Empie and a host of others are at the very forefront of this renewing and reinterpreting experience of the living presence of Christ. Theologians such as Joseph Sittler, Jaroslav Pelikan, Taito A. Kantonnen, Kristen E. Skydsgaard, Kristen Stendhal, George Linbeck share vigorously in the ecumenical dialogue. To name these few is but a suggestion of the many who participate on every front of the contemporary scene. It is a strong faith in God that motivates their leadership. While the Lutheran may not be optimistic about any organization in the state or in the church being a replica of the kingdom, he is not going to retreat from the encounter.

As noted previously, American Lutherans have expressed their faith in an amazing number of ways. Colleges and seminaries of the highest order, institutions of mercy such as hospitals, convalescent homes, a variety of social service agencies, hundreds of missionaries (who have gone to other continents to help indigenous churches come into existence) experiments in public relations that have caused them to share in all of the mass media of the day—all these are evidences of the lively ferment and sense of commitment which has typified the American translation of the reforming spirit. As Albert Stauderman wrote when the Lutheran Church of America came into existence, "Our ancestors preserved this great heritage when they brought the evangelical faith of the Lutheran Church to the shores of this hemisphere. Our history in the United States and Canada goes back to the achievements of those days, when pioneer fathers and mothers braved the hardships of the frontier and when adventurous preachers and teachers organized the earliest congregations. We cannot be less brave or forward-looking than those of the past. Our new unity brings new opportunities." [3]

Twentieth-century Lutheranism looks more like the dynamic sixteenth-century variety, more like the struggles in the Augustinian period of Christianity, more like those formative days of early Christendom when the signposts were indefinite but the spirit determined. St. Paul insisted that the Christians of Asia Minor were "no longer aliens in a foreign land, but fellow-citizens with God's people, members of God's household. You are built upon the foundation laid by the apostles and prophets, and Christ Jesus himself is the foundation stone. In him the whole building is bonded together and grows into a holy temple in the Lord. In him you, too, are being built with all the rest into a spiritual dwelling for God." (Ephesians 2:19–22) Lutherans understand this and in a remarkable parallel have had to experience this situation in America. This is why the old "expectation" which Luther underscored requires new and hopeful significance in our own time. It is why the Lutheran Churches in America have been erupting into new forms and involving themselves in new situations; uncertain of the emerging shapes but confident that the quest must be continued; certain that ways must be found today to proclaim that God is with us. It is a time of renewal and the ferment of interest in the church in America is a new translation of the spirit of the Reformation. As a member of one of these groups I know how much we need one another. There is a ferment of believing unbelief and unbelieving belief. Lutheranism, is done with any protective stance; it is out on the new frontiers where its heritage of faith demands its witness. Its danger is, in the words of Franklin Clark Fry, "setting the music of our souls exclusively to the metronome of this world so that we lose the strains of eternity. Our Gospel deserves to have the smell of reality but its overriding purpose must not be lost sight of. It is pervasively and effectively to suffuse the whole life of our time. This is our stance." [4]

The Lutheran Churches
In the United States and Canada, 1965:

The Lutheran Church in America	3,265,205
The Lutheran Church-Missouri Synod	2,788,241
The American Lutheran Church	2,587,204
The Lutheran Church-Wisconsin Synod	358,466
The Synod of Evangelical Lutheran Churches	20,464
Church of Lutheran Confession	8,728
The Evangelical Lutheran Synod	14,608
The Apostolic Lutheran Church in America	7,203
Church of Lutheran Brethren	8,204
Eilesen Synod	500
Total	9,058,823

Co-operative Lutheran Agencies:
The Lutheran Council of America (in the process of formation) constituting a federation of Lutheran Churches for co-operative work in various areas. This Council will succeed the National Lutheran Council.

The Lutheran World Federation

72 member churches accounting for 75% of world Lutheranism's 73 million members.

Organized in 1947 the Federation provides a forum and channel of action for the global concerns of this international agency of Protestants.

XI

The Whole Man:
Faith in Many Forms

Come, Holy Spirit, God and Lord;
Be all thy gifts in plenty poured
To save, to strengthen and make whole
Each ready mind, each waiting soul.
O, by the brightness of thy light
In holy faith all men unite.
And to thy praise, by every tongue,
In every land, our hymn be sung.
Alleluia! Alleluia!

—*M. Luther*

Modern man is aware that he lives in a split-up world. He is afraid of a power that could blow it up. He is attacked daily by all kinds of pressures that threaten to fragment. He is involved in schedules which leave him wondering about the meaning of it all. He is a person, but he finds it difficult to think of himself as a whole person. As a Christian he knows that this person-hood is a reality. He finds the most important reality in Christ in knowing that he is a redeemed and reconciled person—he is held together.

Dietrich Bonhoeffer once insisted:

The lordship of Christ is not the rule of a foreign power; it is the lordship of the Creator, Reconciler and Redeemer, the lordship of him through whom and for whom all created beings exist, of him indeed all created beings alone find their origin, their goal and their essence! Jesus Christ's claim to lordship, which is proclaimed by the church, means at the same time the emancipation of the family, culture and government for the realization of their own essential character, which has its foundation in Christ.[1]

We are meant to be whole people and that wholeness is not something to be split up in or by the Church. We are in the world and Christ is the Lord of all. It is this holiness that gives wholeness. The reconciliation of a man with the love of God is the understanding that he can be at worship in the daily round. To be a Christian is to have a sense of this wholeness which expresses itself with confidence and freedom.

Prayer · To many Christians, the most free expression of Christian faith is in prayer life. It is here that one finds the conversation with God—in the formality of his worship and in the expression of his daily life. It is all God's and that includes what he does. Paul's "praying unceasingly" makes sense in this understanding of the graciousness of God which must be reflected in a graciousness of the Christian. It is this understanding that causes Bach to write at the head of his music, *Solo Deo Gloria*, which is more than a pious motto; it is a confession of faith that God is the God of all. There is a wholeness that is expressed not only in his chorales but in the intention of the music. This is prayer at its best. When the Christian has joined his fellow Christians in the services of worship and united his prayers with the hurt and cursed of the world in his daily round, he finds something which holds the contrapuntal nature of his life together, giving it intention and purpose. His prayer is, as Luther wrote, "the conversation of a believing heart with God."

The Lutheran Bishop of Bavaria once said, "I was a pastor ministering in a hospital. A patient said to me, 'If you were a ditchdigger, you'd have a more useful calling than you have now.' That was a long time ago but I have

not forgotten it." He went on to say that as he watched
the nurses and the doctors in the important and essential
carrying out of their daily tasks, he understood the need of
this wholeness in life.

The Lutheran has had to learn, as well, that his understanding of Law and Gospel, of nature and grace, is not a
kind of theological splitting up of life, either. God is at
work in both Law and Gospel. He is at work in the church
and the world. He is at work in creation and in redemption.

So the prayers of a man, in whatever situation, become
not the whisperings of a lost or separated person; they are
this linking with the wholeness of God. When we hear
the Word of God, we answer in the words and deeds of
our lives. This is prayer; the response to the Word of God.

Here are two prayers of Luther's, known as morning
and evening prayers, which are the mirror of this wholeness.

In the Morning:
>I give thanks unto thee, Heavenly Father, through Jesus
>Christ, thy dear Son, that thou hast protected me through
>the night from all danger and harm; and I beseech thee to
>preserve and keep me this day also from all sin and evil; that
>in all my thoughts, words and deeds, I may serve and please
>thee. Into thy hands I commend my body and soul and all
>that is mine. Let thy holy angels have charge concerning me,
>that the wicked one have no power over me. Amen.

In the Evening:
>I give thanks unto thee, Heavenly Father, through Jesus
>Christ, thy dear Son, that thou hast this day so graciously
>protected me: and I beseech thee to forgive me all my sins
>and the wrong which I have done and, by thy great mercy,
>defend me from all the perils and dangers of this night. Into
>thy hands I commend my body and soul, and all that is
>mine. Let thy holy angels have charge concerning me, that
>the wicked one have no power over me. Amen.

There is not only a simplicity of spirit here but a trust
that is aware of the whole gamut of life. At the end of

the evening prayer Luther wrote, "And then lie down in peace and sleep." This advice is not the pious statement of one who withdraws from life. It is the awareness of the world, the flesh and the Devil—and the reconciling love of God! It is an inner-directed spirit from the sixteenth century speaking to the troubled, sensation-seeking and anxiety-ridden, other-directed person in the twentieth century.

The collects or prayers which have been brought together in the *Lutheran Service Book and Hymnal* are filled with this sense of wholeness and holiness. They represent a catholicity of Christian experience. Here in one sentence is a prayer poured out with a sense of understanding of this response to God's word:

Let the design of thy great love lighten upon the waste of our wraths and sorrows; and give peace to thy Church, peace among the nations, peace in our dwellings and peace in our hearts; through thy Son, Jesus Christ, Our Lord.

To discover the Lutheran way of life is to understand this ability to be free to share the Word of God, to respond to the Word of God and to express the Word of God in the whole of life. Prayer is the expression of this response not just in a solitary way or a separated piety. It is in the whole of life.

Music • Another facet of this understanding of God's wholeness drenching life is in a Lutheran attitude toward music. Music has been outlawed from some churches and tolerated by others. For Luther music was God's word proclaimed. He placed music next to theology. He insisted that the devil could not stand melodious music. He urged his friends to strike the keys with a will and to sing out. As a result congregational singing became the mark of the Protestant churches. The Lutheran chorales became the distinctive splendor of the congregation, a tie with the past, a fellowship with the present but always a response of the heart and mind to God.

From this delight with music and this understanding of the response to God's power came the long processional of musicians, notably Johann Sebastian Bach and his followers, who have given to life an ecstatic statement of the joy of the Christian faith. Music was an integral part of worship. In the church it proclaimed the Gospel. It wasn't just a nice thing to fit into a program or a solo just in order to give someone a chance to sing. Its hymns, its anthems and its music became worship. A real Lutheran church has real congregational singing.

The congregational singing of the Reformation period was not unique. They were singing songs in the first-century church and the Psalms were the hymnody of a Hebraic tradition. Yet Luther re-introduced hymnody into the church and it has remained an impressive part of the Lutheran experience. In the twentieth century this tradition bids fair to become one of the areas which offers the encouragement of ecumenical respect, an atmosphere of song that can encourage the larger areas of discussion and understanding. The recent adoption of Luther's *A Mighty Fortress Is Our God* by Roman Catholics in numerous services hopefully suggests that we praise God together and not think of Lutheran or Catholic hymns. This is right and proper, for the hymnal itself is a cherished treasure of the witness of the Gospel for all cultural environments, religious traditions and dogmatic assertions. When we sing, even in the difficult moments, we do one of the easiest of the Christian expressions of response, helping the church as well as its members to become whole.

The *Lutheran Service Book and Hymnal* is based on standards which include good hymns for the full round of the Christian year and the Christian life, devotional rather than homiletic, directed Godward instead of manward, ecumenical in character expressing the catholicity and continuity of the church. The editors for the *Lutheran Service Book and Hymnal* stated the purpose of the book, which is important to the individual worshipper: "We share the rich endowments of a common faith, a common history, a common heritage of liturgy and hymnody and the recognition of a common mission and destiny. This book will contribute to the unity of our Church and to the advent of the day when Henry Melchior Muhlenberg's vision of 'one church and one book' will become a reality." [2]

Music is the expression of the Word of God. Sidney Lanier once called music "love in search of a word." It is this yearning to share the heartbeat of mankind in response to his predicament, his joy and his yearning as he expresses the meaning of the Gospel. The new emphasis on congregational singing which has come to Roman Catholicism gives new hope that there may be a possibility of the understanding of our Christian unity. Oswald Spengler once asserted that Roman Catholicism's contribution to art was in the field of painting and Protestantism's in the field of music. If this is true, a large part of the credit is due the genius of Luther who opened the avenues for this expression of man's spirit in praise of his Lord. The names of Heinrich Schütz, Buxtehude, Johann Sebastian Bach, Crüger, Hassler, Nicolai, Frank, Teschner, Albert, Neumark and others highlight the processional of those who contributed to this vast heritage of Lutheran music.

Dr. Luther Reed, the eminent scholar and liturgist, summed up the importance of music in the worship life of the church saying, "The Lutheran Reformation was marked by the triumphant restoration of popular participation in the services, by a great increase in the number of communicants, and by an outburst of liturgical prayer, congregational song and choral music of astonishing quality and extent. The reform of the liturgy and of liturgical worship released newly-awakened powers of individuals and of the Church as a whole. Public worship in exercising and developing the finest, the most spiritual powers of the Body of Christ, appeals to the best in all men. Individuals who could not be interested in doctrinal discussions or even in practical Christian activities are impressed by sincere acts of corporate worship." [3]

This is a facet of the concern of the Christian faith with the whole person. Thus the music and the hymns are not for the sake of these expressions of the human spirit. They express the sense of God's living presence and they speak into the joys, the angers, the hatreds, the boredom and the loves of the present. Bach's glorias can then exalt and indict. Listen to Bach's "St. Matthew's Passion" and you hear the Gospel of grace alone!

Richard Luecke correctly insists, "Worshippers do not bring this song to the church. They find it there. In one sense, one never brings his own songs to church, whether a marching song or the blues or a nymph-and-shepherd number, depending on his mood. One no more chooses the song he sings in church than he chooses the one with whom he sings it. The Church has a song to sing and a man and his neighbor are invited to join in that song. They may not feel like singing it. Such a song may seem inappropriate in a world like this. That was the question of Israel in exile! 'How can we sing the Lord's song in a strange land?' Yet this is exactly what the church is required to do . . . The song of the church is not based on ordinary human accomplishments or feelings or fellow-feelings, but on a deed of grace already accomplished in the world and for the world." [4]

Art and Architecture · This theological insistence that God's presence bursts through, creating forms and meaning in myriads of ways, finds particular expression in art and architecture. The shape of the church building and the art used to express the faith of the worshipper are part and parcel of the body of belief. The faith expressed in times past and communicating to the present should give integrity to the art and architecture of the local parish. That this is not always so is an indication of our unwillingness to express the faith we accept. Men are often willing to subsidize what they will not imitate! There is a quality of security that ought to enable congregations to speak this faith with the freedom that breaks from copying one's neighbors. It is tragic to lose the excitement of the Gospel either through dull conformity to tradition or indulgence in something whimsical just to be contemporary. There is an integrity in the whole of life. What a man believes ought to be apparent in that expression and celebration of his faith. Dr. Edward Frey delightfully states, "Our buildings must bristle with belief or they fail to advance the Christian witness in the midst of the smog of secularism which has settled down so rapidly over present-day communities. So we say, 'Think before you build.' " [5] He might have added that as a slogan for the expression of faith in any activity. Our beliefs ought to motivate the shape of our buildings—for that matter, the shape of our lives!

In other words, Lutherans—as well as others—need to consider their faith when designing their buildings. It has been a just boast that this theological insistence is expressing itself in the architecture of the church. It is a way in which the Lutheran community can indicate a continuing contribution to the development of this "form of content." The architecture is a symbol of the life and program.

In this context Dr. Edgar Brown comments, "The church is not an ad hoc assembly, created especially for this gathering of the people at a particular time in a particular place. It enjoys a history, and so has a heritage. The marks of this heritage are a part of its life. Because at one time the church spoke Greek, the liturgy still prefers to label its opening litany "Kyrie." Latin terms still survive as brief yet adequate titles for many portions of liturgical expressions, not to mention theological explication. Vestments in use today are not greatly unlike those worn 1500 years ago, and the same can be said for ceremonies, rites and furnishings." [6]

Simply, there is a catholicity of this theological faith, a way of thinking about God and his wonderful works, which sets in motion the expression of man's emotions and is seen in all that he shapes.

Evangelism and Stewardship · Evangelism, the witness of the living Word, and stewardship, the responsible use of the whole of life, energy and resources, are in a very real sense a public proclamation of the Gospel. It is a strange distortion that enables churches to have people who claim membership as if in a kind of private club, in which there is a kind of cultural uniformity, to which they pay dues, but through which they fail to express any commitment.

The Reformation was a reaction to a type of stylizing of churchmanship into rigid forms. The continuing reformation of our own time is a rethinking of the manner in which the Word is made accessible to mankind. True freedom implies responsibility. Contemporary Christianity is involved in a rethinking of its stategy in a pluralistic culture. It cannot be satisfied with gimmicks. It cannot be content with the all-too-frequent public image of a group of people engaged in superficial events, raising money in a variety of ways to support an institution.

Because of this, Lutheran churches have been insistent that the work of the church be supported by free-will gifts and offerings. The local congregation cannot become a competitor to local business nor can fund-raising become a substitute piety. The work of the kingdom is not financed by bazaars. In recent conventions stewardship commissions have made statements that seem extreme in their detailing of this philosophy. They run the risk of a kind of Pharisaism, a boasting of what is not done. Obviously, the test is in what the congregation is doing. It thrusts it back upon its own confession of vocation, asking that the responsive love be shown in the practical activities of the management of the local congregation, and risking its own corporate life in a new forgetfulness.

Faith is shared in many forms and in the practicalities of every day. Luther stated it in his Preface to Romans. "Faith is not human day-dreaming which some people confuse with it. 'Faith does not suffice,' they say, 'we must also do good deeds if we are to be religious and truly blessed.' But true faith is a work of God in us which transforms and regenerates us by the power of God, slays the old Adam and makes us men whose hearts and faculties are entirely renewed by the Holy Spirit. Oh, it is a living, energizing, active, powerful thing—this faith. That it should not be ceaselessly active for good is just impossible. It does not ask whether there are good works to be done; for, before one can ask, it has already done them . . . It is always in action. One can no more separate works from faith than one can separate light and heat from flame." [7]

Evangelism and stewardship are the light and the heat that cannot be separated from the flame of this love of God. Try to separate it and you have gimmicks, programs and a loss of spirit.

This is good Christianity, underscored in Luther's reforming principle, which needs to be renewed in the context of the exciting new world of 450 years later. To worship God in spirit is the service and honor of the heart. It

comprehends faith and fear in God. The worshipping of
God is two-fold, outward and inward—that is to acknowledge God's benefits and to be thankful unto him. Recognizing this we listen especially to the words of a Roman
Catholic layman of our generation who says, "A Church
made up of men and women who do not know the demands of honesty within the Church cannot be expected
to resist the dishonesties of society. A Christian who cannot enter into an honest relationship with himself will
find it difficult to enter into an honest relationship with
others. A Church which does not encourage and provide
the conditions necessary for honesty cannot expect to gain
the perception of itself required of its mission." [8] He was
writing for his own tradition, but he writes for us all. We
Lutherans have proclaimed this certainty of the Christian
faith. Now we must find new ways to testify to this forgiving, healing, redeeming relationship in what we are,
what we do, what we willingly and honestly share in the
complexities of today's urgencies. We may not find immediate statistics to support such evangelism and stewardship; we will find the joy of Christian vocation.

The Whole · There is no place in the Christian experience for a kind of split-level morality, with the spiritual
holding sway on one floor and the profane on the other.
A similar battle was fought in the sixteenth century and
needs a present-day interpretation. Having confessed it in
our statements of faith, we need to live it out in the climate of our acts. The denial of this fact has made the
man of faith vulnerable to the attacks of the "God is
dead" terminology. It attacks the "God in a particular
place." The spatial beyond is destroyed; the real presence
ought now to be more clearly recognized.

It is the whole person that is involved, as is the whole
world. This is inherent in the Protestant statement and,

when it is an inherent in the Christian way of life, it will best express that for which the reformers fought centuries ago. They had to break out of the monasteries to insist upon the valid work of God in the wholeness of the world; in our time there is the same temptation to dimension Christianity and isolate it from "the world."

It may be more comfortable for us to enter some "monastery" of urban anonymity; but that is not the calling of the Christian. He is called to witness as a whole person. This recognition will lead him into an area which has been one of Lutheranism's most difficult; namely, his call to speak of politics and social action. Yet it is as much a part of the call as is the call to the piety of prayer, the harmony of music and the capturing of a hint of the eternal.

After the resurrection we are told that "the doors being shut, Jesus was with them." It is this breakthrough that has never quite made the impact upon the Christian that one might have suspected. Men are always closing big doors upon certain areas of life as though they could effectively rule God out. To accept Christianity in truth is to effectively deny that death can rule God out. There is a catholicity and universality of Protestantism which is the new evangelical witness of the "real presence." The Lutheran way of life is concerned with the whole man in the whole of life.

XII

The World of the Christian:
The Voice of Conscience

> With thee there is forgiveness, Lord,
> And love and grace abounding;
> The noblest thought and deed and word
> Were else but empty sounding.
> All guilty in thy sight appear;
> All to thy presence come in fear,
> And find thy lovingkindness.
> —M. Luther

The church is always searching for the way in which to be the voice of the prophet and the reconciling healer in society. There were days when the church could serve as a haven, a refuge and a sanctuary. Now the Christian community is trying to discover the new urgencies of its being as "a royal priesthood, a holy nation, God's chosen people." How shall the people of God live in this kind of a world? What are the clear ethical directives? How shall we find selfhood in this community? Confronted by wars, declared or undeclared, seeing clearly the complexities of urban life, alive to the pressures of the political struggle, and determined to be a channel of God's love, Christians find it difficult indeed to "render unto Caesar the things that are Caesar's and unto God the things that are God's." (Matthew 22:21)

The Reformation was a rebirth of a New Testament theological insistence, born in an age which was justifying means by ends in the same way in which prudential ethics are rationalized today. For Luther, only faith could guarantee ethical action. We are citizens of two kingdoms, we belong to both of them. A Christian simply cannot escape either his membership in the family of God or his obligations to society. Nonetheless, he can insulate himself with his pieties as though he were still asking, Am I my brother's keeper? Luther said that we ought to be Christs to one another. If he were writing today he would command us to recognize the Christ in our neighbor. This is the theological basis for action, the vocation that cuts across all artificial divisions, until we look more like the living community of our living Lord. "What are the good works you are to do to your neighbor? Answer, they have no name . . . Thus it is not your good work that you shall give alms or pray but that you offer yourself to your neighbor and serve him, wherever he needs you and every way you can, be it with alms, prayer, work, fasting, counsel, comfort, instruction, admonition, punishment, apologizing, clothing, food, and lastly with suffering and dying for him." [1]

The importance of such recognition is that there is no identification of humanitarianism as the final measurement; the goodness is in the recognition of the love of God in my neighbor. This recognition founded institutions of mercy and motivated social protests. In the earlier discussions of the abolition of sacred and secular there is the foundation for discovering the Word of God in both civil and ecclesiastical—in the world as well as in the church. In a time when the church asserted its supremacy over the state, Luther protested. In another age when the state insisted that the church become its slave, Lutheranism protested. Yet, in quiet times, it has been a complex problem for Lutheranism to understand the relation of church and state and to discover its function as a conscience to society.

John Wesley wrote in 1738 that it was a reading of

Luther's "Preface to the Romans" that warmed his heart
and started the movement known as the Methodist
Church. In this century it ought to be a sharing of that
same grappling with the meaning of the Gospel that
would cause a new warming of the heart in our secularized
world.

Two Kingdoms • The New Testament discusses the state
as divinely ordained, insisting that the power of the state
is of God for the maintenance of peace and justice. Church
and State were separated by the Reformation; their relation is in tension today. "Accordingly Christians are
obliged to be subject to civil authority and obey its commands and laws in all that can be done without sin. But
when commands of the civil authority cannot be obeyed
without sin, we must obey God rather than man." (Acts
5:29) [2] There have been those who blamed Lutherans for
silence concerning Hitlerism insisting that such teaching
permitted Christians to refrain from protest while atroc-
ities were perpetrated. Nothing could be farther from the
truth. If this were done, it would be a distortion of this
teaching. It is Luther's teaching that God is the Lord of
all and, therefore, there can be no dualism. It is not possible to act one way in one Kingdom, and another way in
the other Kingdom—they exist together. A Christian
knows that God demands more of him than does the
state; that the man of Christ goes the seventh mile; that
love is always operative in the search for righteousness and
justice.[3]

Joseph Sittler rightly insists that our problem in contemporary society is in our covert idolization of values as
we attempt to find a form of godliness to uphold the situation. "If God is sought in order to integrate the personality, the actual God is not God but the integrated
personality. And when men are urged to renovate their

religious values in order that the Republic may be the more firmly glued together, this covert idolatry reaches a peculiarly pernicious and untruthful pitch. There is a relation between a people who are blessed because their God is the Lord, but one does not find it recorded that God the Lord consents to be compounded into political glue." [4] This is the underscoring of the Lutheran insistence that it is why and how we act that determines the worth of what we do. It is in Christ in whom we move and live and have our being. "God is in Christ reconciling the world to himself."

The Inter-related Kingdoms · This places the responsibility of the Christian in its proper relationship. Luther insisted that God does not need our acts of love. Our neighbor does. The failure to meet the need is a condemnation of the quietism and withdrawal that has so frequently typified congregational life. To Luther it was impossible that a congregation should worship, sing hymns, teach the Gospel and then withdraw from this sense of responsibility. There were two kingdoms but they were God's kingdoms and they were inter-related. "The Christian acts in society because he knows that it is in the living community that God wants to be served." [5] The church has been typified as the interfering community. So it is, if by interference one means the insistence that the Christian searches for the word of God on the issue and acts out his role in the midst of the scene. If the church is a backwater crowd of quietists who are afraid of the world or withdrawn from the neighborhood, it has missed the very thrust of Lutheranism's understanding of the Gospel.

There is no easy way to determine when to obey God rather than men. The countless, nameless Christians who have stood against their own governments know that cost. The "holy worldliness" that Bonhoeffer underscored is the

insistence that there not be a rigid separation, or a dimen-
sioning of righteousness. When the church "sticks to the
Gospel," we are involved in the whole of life. This is the
contribution Lutherans could make to the present crises.
In the racial tensions, economic and social upheavals, in
the struggle to find other ways than wars to settle international issues, we are dealing with the values men really
hold. The Gospel sets the foundation for these decisions.
We can say, "Our Father who art in heaven," but it is not
so evident whether God is really alive in the lives of those
who call on Him. When Luther insisted on removing the
easy line between sacred and secular and called on men to
see the whole of the world of man as God's world, he set
men free. If modern Lutherans have not always used that
freedom, they only intensify the dilemma of the situation.
The creative God calls his people to be responsible ministers
in this strange new world.

The whole issue was never more clearly illustrated than
at the 1964 Convention of the Lutheran Church in America. One of the Boards of the church had presented a series
of resolutions that went to the core of the sin of racial
prejudice. Included in its statements were the following
words: "In the Prayer of the Church we petition: 'Give
to all men the mind of Christ and dispose our days in thy
peace, O God. Take from us all hatred and prejudice, and
whatever may hinder unity of spirit and concord!' These
sentences are related. Our days cannot be lived in God's
peace unless hatred and prejudice are removed from us.
The prayer is realistic; it recognizes that we are guilty of
harboring hatreds and prejudices which we are inclined to
hold dear . . . To stand before God and pray that 'he
will take from us all hatred and prejudice' and then as a
praying church to discriminate among men on any such
sinful basis is an act of blasphemy."

The debate that followed the reading indicated how

difficult it is for some men of good will, even in these days, to discover that which is basic in their own faith; namely, that God is the God of all. To deny this is blasphemous. To acknowledge this is to discover the inter-relatedness of these kingdoms of which Luther spoke. Nothing in God's creation is profane or God-forsaken. Everything is subject to and open to this rule and love of God. On such a basis, whatever the label, the evangelical witness of the New Testament can be set free in the world. This requires faith but that is the gift which, in the end, is the source of strength and the assurance of justification.

"All things are yours . . . and you are Christ's; and Christ is God's," wrote St. Paul. (1 Cor. 3:22) On that basis there is a new freedom and incentive to belong to all, in their sins, their burdens, their triumphs, their needs. Some of the finest exploration of Lutherans—as well as all others of the Christian community—is going to be in the laboratory of sharing this "faith alone," "grace alone" witness as the basis of meeting the hurts and needs of mankind. It is still true, that just as we are not saved by our works, so we are not freed from fruitage. "By their fruits you shall know them," is the injunction of Jesus. Here in this faith and love, is the hope the Christian brings in a new identification with his brother.

Inner Missions · The principle of being Christs one to another is illustrated dramatically in the social welfare movement of compassion and concern that developed within the church. Known as Inner Missions, it took literally the command of Jesus to feed the poor, comfort the widows and care for the orphans. The forerunners of what so many of us take for granted in the world of today was born in the pietism of the Pfliedners and Frankes and others who founded institutions of mercy. The modern nurse remembers Florence Nightingale who was influenced by the work of these pioneer Lutheran institutions. These were the days when the church was the center of an aroused conscience which expressed itself in the institutions and hospitals where compassion was literally practiced. The idea spread to America in the nineteenth century and such leaders as Passavant expanded this work of mercy. The list of Lutheran institutions of mercy is impressive. To a large extent these agencies were locally inspired; the responsibility resting in the agency itself.

In order to care for the sick and also serve in congregations, communities, and homes, a Deaconess movement grew and developed. Thousands of women going about in their uniforms (which marked them as members of the Diaconate) became the familiar scene in Protestant Germany and Scandinavia. The movement has never been as widespread in the United States and Canada but it has contributed an influence which continues and is in another period of renewal. In an age which is discovering anew the sense of mission and commitment, these earlier explorers of diakonia lighted the way. Their "holy worldliness" was lived out within the accustomed structures. It may be that out of that same diaconate idea the new sense of living beyond the accustomed structures of the church and expressing concern in the whole of life will find a new impetus.

In another century this urgency established institutions in local neighborhoods and in far-off countries. Long before such familiar government agencies as "Peace Corps," these Lutherans were exploring the deeper meanings of community. All of this grew out of a theological certainty which erupted into hospitals, schools, social agencies, and a whole host of compassionate ministries. It was an institutionalized ministry but it served and met needs in its own day. Lutherans in our time are trying to confront the new forms of the city where the adventure is not so easily in-

stitutionalized. In a time where there is much doubt as to
the structures of the parish and in which there is also
much theological turmoil, there is a clarity in reading the
statement of Luther, "God's word is the beginning of all;
on it follows faith and on faith charity." This was the basis
of public piety. It was a holy piety as long as it did not
shrivel into a private piety that tried to ignore the world.
Today there is a new responsibility to exercise this witness
and initiative in this social revolution.

The Social Struggle · It isn't enough to be compassionate
to the victims of society; one has to deal with the environment that creates the victims. Bonhoeffer justified his return to Germany during the Nazi period because he said
it wasn't enough to stand on the side of the street while a
madman drove a car which was slaughtering people. You
couldn't stand on the sidelines and decry what was happening; you had to get into the street and stop the car.

At the point of "car-stopping," the Lutherans in America
have not always been notable. That can be explained by a
concern with cultural and language problems and with an
inherent desire not to measure faith by works. There was
a shying from the old forms of the social Gospel. Lutherans
were cautious, and sometimes antagonistic, to forms of
social action. Yet the problems persisted and none of
these alert Lutheran congregations hide from them. In the
past forty years there has been an impressive list of public statements with bold and creative witnessing in the
area of social ministry. Brave stands have been taken concerning the sins of racial tensions, the problems of home
and marriage, the relation of church and state, religious
liberty and the problems of labor and management. The
Lutheran believes in the separation of church and state,
yet he knows that he cannot live in some Lutheran ghetto,
isolated from the world, or insulated from the heats and

passions of mankind. It is his involvement too. That involvement is not only the result of his sin: it is also the presence of the Holy Spirit. It is knowing that God is in it all and no one can retreat. The power of God can be known anywhere. Understanding this power rescues man from refighting sixteenth-century battles. The church is free to challenge and influence decisions now. Preaching the Word and administering the Sacraments is basic, and not limited to the pulpit and altar. Therefore the believer is out in the world where the grace that he knows and receives in word and sacrament are active in dealing with the dilemmas of man. The church has a responsibility not only for its own members but also for the community!

Dr. William Lazareth has suggested steps which the church can take in fulfilling this imperative:

1. The church can encourage qualified and consecrated laymen to make government service the occupational expression of their Christian vocation.
2. The church can conduct serious discussions among its members in the analysis of domestic affairs and international relations from a distinctively Christian perspective.
3. The church can strive to create a moral and legal climate of opinion at HOME and throughout the world in which solutions to vexing political problems can take place more easily.
4. The church (or any one of its official agencies such as the Commission of the Churches on International Affairs) can proclaim the general norms and guidelines of Christian political ethics in order to provide judgment and guidance for those responsible under God for peace, justice, and freedom of the world.[6]

These are some of the positive actions that can be taken by the local congregation as it fulfills its function as a body of believing people.

The problem most Lutherans confront is that they recognize the risk in all of this. One is subject to criticism, to judgment and to the possibility of making a human mistake. But to do nothing is also to vote. No Christian who takes his heritage seriously can be content to remain inside the structure of the congregation while he confesses allegiance to a faith which broke through structures centuries ago and talked of the love of God which reconciles the whole of mankind. The Lutheran may make mistakes but they won't be the error of a lack of responsibility. Our very freedom gives us the privilege of "bearing one another's burdens."

Personal and Social · Basic to all of this is the Lutheran insistence upon the rebirth of the individual. Just patching up things, or moving a few prejudices around won't do. Salvation requires rebirth or renewal. It is this "new Adam" which was a basic understanding of God's living grace. The tragedy is that in too many situations this fundamental doctrine has been overlooked or neglected. What this Lutheran actually confesses is that he is subject to both law and Gospel. That drives him into a new relationship with the whole of life. His comfort and his strength is in the knowledge of the grace that gives him security in the midst of the danger and graciousness in the expression of his faith. He knows that God cares for him; out of this love grows his own caring enough to do something about it.

If the church is to express the conscience of the Christian faith it will be by the rebirth of the individual and the expression of a faith that tackles the issues in society. His certainty is in the fact that God loved the world. That is more significant than specific codes of action which are situational and relative. That love was so great that his basic understanding of the atoning love of Christ is centered just here. God loved the world, so he gave his son. It is in this reconciling act, basic to Paul and to Luther, that the contemporary Lutheran finds a burst into a new theological understanding and a new social responsibility. The Christian is here not to moralize, nor to be judgmental but to be gracious and loving, bringing adequate witness to the healing power of God.

To be Lutheran in the expression of this Christianity is to understand this knowledge, in consonance with his fellows everywhere as citizens and churchmen, to share this good news in action as well as announcement. Stated simply and clearly in Luther's definition of the First Commandment: "We are to fear, to love and to trust in God above all things." That's revolutionary.

Perhaps the most exciting laboratories of all of this are in the life of congregations all across America. Here imaginative and dedicated members are joining in the day by day experiences of relating the love of God to the hurts in their own neighborhoods and doing it with an optimism leaping from faith. The Gospel is being shared in social action, in practical dealing with social ills, in reconciling groups and renewing neighborhoods, in coffee houses and jazz ministries, in the witness that demonstrates that we must love and trust God above all things. That's still revolutionary and it is in the life and work of many of our local congregations that this crisis is best understood. In the end, all of this is really sharing the Word and the Sacraments and there is a voice of conscience sounding above the outrage and the apathy of the world.

XIII

Steeples in the Struggle:
Lutheranism in the Contemporary Dialogue

> Lord Jesus Christ, thy power make known
> For thou art Lord of lords alone;
> Defend thy Christendom, that we
> May evermore sing praise to thee.
> —*M. Luther*

A few generations ago steeples punctuated the American landscape. You came over the crest of the hill to see the village nestled in the valley, its tallest symbol the steeple of the church. The skyline of the burgeoning city had a variety of these churchly spires. Now, in so many instances, they are gone or dwarfed. What has happened architecturally is but a symbol of that which is happening to the thinking in our culture. Every institution is being subjected to tests and pressure and that includes the church. Inside and outside the church there are harsh critics. There is a kind of smart jargon, almost a fad, that spoofs at the parish, explains its vulnerability and predicts its doom. There is enough evidence to give rise to the assertion.

If the local parish of any denomination finds itself in such a dilemma, it becomes but the specific symbol of the larger witness of the denomination. The local steeple is a symbol of that larger edifice. All of which raises the logical question, What does the Lutheran steeple suggest in today's turmoil?

The evangelical witness was born as a lively reform and, above all others, it ought to be most sensitive to renewal. Such reform cannot remain true to the faith and then be subject to the pressures of society. If that ever happened then the church would be untrue to its very nature. Its own statements proclaim a faith based beyond the pressure. The ability of men of courage to stand against the social pressures of their day attests to this power to withstand the external pressure. The church proclaims itself as the witness of the "good news" which sets it apart from the possibility of absorption into the landscape. Yet any honest observer knows that this is easier said than done. To preach the Word and share the sacraments with contemporary man places the people of God in the midst of the tensions where faith must be re-examined every day.

Beyond this the Lutheran finds himself in the ferment of an ecumenical situation which moves rapidly toward the requirement to act as we have prayed. Through the centuries the prayer of the church has been:

Save and defend thy Church universal, purchased with the precious blood of Christ. Give it pastors and ministers, according to thy Spirit, and strengthen it through the Word and the holy Sacraments. Make it perfect in love and in all good works, and establish it in the faith delivered to the saints. Sanctify and unite thy people in all the world, that one holy Church may bear witness to thee, the God and Father of all; we beseech thee to hear us, good Lord.

That prayer, shared by Lutheran worshippers, must now be sustained by the life and action of Lutheran parishioners.

If Lutherans require others to adopt the form of the statements of faith which have been the continuing heritage of the Lutheran group, they are untrue to their own confessions of faith. The confessions stated that "it is enough to agree upon the Word and the sacraments" in order to discover this sense of unity. These Confessions insist that the Scriptures furnish the source of our unity. The same spirit of the New Testament that Lutherans such as Söderblom, and scholars and leaders of our time, have given and continue to share gives encouragement to the whole Christian family. Just as in international affairs, nations have had to move from dependence, through independence, to interdependence; so these families of the family of God move into a new sense of unity.

In this spirit the Lutheran family comes with its heritage and its experience. To cut itself off from its history would be to become a kind of truncated development, not really catholic in its experience. To hide itself in its solitary struggle in the sixteenth century would be untrue to the Gospel which flows through its movement. It was born to communicate that living Word. When it does, it is evangelical, sharing the good news, and communicating this word in the midst of the present experience. When Bonhoeffer discussed the ecumenical movement and the Confessing Church, he raised many questions that all members of the Christian family confront. He urged an ecumenical council which would be able "to bear witness against the enemies of Christianity throughout the world, whether it will speak a word of judgment about war, race hatred and social exploitation, whether through such true ecumenical unity of all evangelical Christians among all nations war itself will become impossible, whether the witness of such a council will find ears to hear—all this depends on our obedience towards the question which has been put to us and on the way in which God will use our obedience. What is set up is not an ideal, but a command and a promise—what is demanded is not our own realization of our own aims, but obedience. The question has been raised." [1] Indeed it has.

The problem must be confronted not only by the theologians and the strong leaders of our national and international bodies. It must be answered by the members of the local congregation. It is in the local neighborhood, the local community, the labor union, the community organization and in the school districts and also in the theological dialogue that the witness of this faith is known. To disown that responsibility is, somehow, to expect that an international agency can determine the entire situation. Obviously the larger agency can set the tone. It cannot do more. It must be in the local parish that this quality of daring, this specific particularity of the spirit is known.

It is one thing to proclaim a resolution concerning racial tension. It is another thing when a congregation takes a stand, dares the possibility of social jeopardy in the local community and decides to be obedient to this evangelical witness. It is one thing to assert a concern for housing; it is another thing when a local Lutheran congregation takes its stand with other citizens to insist on local housing codes. This witness is a faith shared, creating a mood and a climate. It is not that it is unique; it is specific and particular, certain that it knows what it is about and quite willing to take the risk of sharing its evangelical tradition in a continuing, renewing and reforming liveliness. Martin Marty looked at these same skylines and wrote, "The church has inhaled; now it exhales. It withdrew: now it attacks. The cathedral is overtowered by the skyscrapers in the modern city; so, no longer will the tall towers of romantic Christendom prevail. The church bears a substantive, not a dimensional reference to the city. It must have something to say and a way to live. Here the effects of catechetics, teaching, liturgical and edifying preaching will be tested. A sermon should not be preached in a church but in the city, said Luther in a church. Kierkegaard said: 'Take Luther up on it; move out into the city.' "[2]

Where will the Lutheran draw some of this underscoring in the ecumenical and urban discussion? Having told a bit of the story, what is worth sharing abroad?

The Lordship of Christ · The emphasis first of all is its understanding of the Christian witness. The reforming spirit caught this note and echoed it in times past. It was the good news. It refused to allow anything in orders, forms, powers or precepts to overshadow that steeple. To speak of the centrality of Christ was not just to suggest a pious cliché. It was to insist that in a time when men discuss volubly the death of God, there must be raised the living witness of God as men have known the "Word become flesh." To have caught that spirit is to have security in ecumenical discussions, courage in social boldness, peace in the tempest. The missionary who said, "For me to live is Christ," had discovered that inner witness. "Revelation," writes Paul Scherer, "is the fusion under God of fact with ultimate meaning, event with Word." [3]

It is this lordship which gives new meaning to the Sacraments. This is the real presence. There is no denominational dimension here. It breaches the walls that traditions and cultural barriers erect and expresses a lively witness. It is not just what Christ said or did. It is what He is that is the clue to the meaning of existence. The entire deed of God in Christ for man's redemption is present here.

The secularization of so much of the culture of mankind bleeds vocation from life. To those who have kept a Christocentric understanding, there is grace that secures against fright. It is the faith in Christ the transformer—to use Richard Niebuhr's phrase. "This Christ has a history, he is remembered and he is expected. This Christian has a history of relations to Christ; he remembers his denials and mistaken interpretations of Christ's words. The Christian is a member of a company which has a history of re-

lations to him and to Christ. To be contemporaneous with
Christ is to be contemporaneous with one who was present
to Augustine as well as to Paul, and is in the presence of
the least of his brothers." [4] In that community there is a
faith that doesn't despair.

In the dialogue of this moment it is imperative that the
knowledge of the life, of and in Christ, be understood and
known. The critics aver that the church has little effect on
our value systems. The pressures on modern man are
subtle and mighty. In whatever discussion the Christian
finds himself, there must be the fact that he is Christ's.
It is this renewing faith which is the reforming dynamic.
"I believe that Jesus Christ, true God, begotten of the
Father from eternity and true man, born of the virgin
Mary is my Lord; who has redeemed me . . ." That is a
sentence to underscore in the contemporary situation.

Faith That Holds · The man of faith lives in a time when
the word "faith" seems to indicate an intellectual exercise.
Contemporary man has enough burdens to pick up without trying to add others. Faith seems to be another load
instead of a supporting strength. So it is a time of un-faith
instead of a faith-full time.

For Luther, faith was something to which a man could
cling. To be justified by faith was to understand both the
cold edge of the law and the warm grace of love. You
could not win that. You could not decide it on your own.
You went out to the edges of your mind and you trusted.
You could confront the infinity of this universe and the
cybernetics of this new age, with the certainty that nothing
could separate you from the meaning of life as sacred. It
is this liberating quality of faith which gets overlooked too
often. Faith becomes equated with dogmas or an inven-
tory of assents or with a kind of moralistic "thou shalt" and
"thou shalt not." To Jesus it was fulfilling the law until you

moved out into a new dimension of flavor and light. The danger in the present is that the steeples we erect seem to be a proud assemblage of beliefs instead of stalwart certainty to which a man can cling. When some men proclaim an atheism in order to discover an ethical optimism they miss this meaning of faith. To believe is to trust—that's enough security for the adventure.

Security—and risk too—enables a man to fulfill his vocation as a person. To be justified by faith is to be a whole person in this kind of world. In the struggle for the allegiances of mankind and in the whole revolution of values and ideals in our world, this faith that can strip the masks from man leaves him with hope instead of despair. "The good things we have received from God should flow from one to another" wrote Luther, "and be common to all, so that everyone should put on his neighbor and so conduct himself toward him as if he himself were in the other's place." This is what it means to be free. This is inherent in the sanctifying and justifying grace that the Lutheran talks about and, hopefully, lives by. God has reconciled the world unto himself. This knowledge gives meaning to life. We need its emphasis just now.

Communicating the Word · The steeple of translation bulks large on the skyline. Luther was insistent that the words should be set free from Latin so that the Word should be free in the minds of people. That heroic work of translation has been a significant hallmark of Lutheranism, a pride in times past and a prod to contentment with forms in our own time. To be a member of the Lutheran Church is to know of this urgency to communicate through translation. It is to accept the proposition that there is something to communicate, an idea that can't be imprisoned in language or in forms. It may break loose from the old form but it doesn't abandon it. Because Luther wanted the Bible translated into German he did not negate the meaningful place of Latin. Communication is always a translation into a new form at that particular moment.

The genius of translation is to work into the word and then allow that word to speak. The translator then gets out of the way. To understand this factor in the Reformation period is to catch a glimpse of a contribution in our own time. Jesus said that men of faith were to be salt and light. The salt in itself was not the important fact; it was what it brought out. The original inherent flavor is set loose. It is only when the church allows that saltiness to be at work that it fulfills its useful place in society. It is there that it translates the good news from the Latin of institutionalized forms and ancient verbiage into the warmth of contemporary language that men understand. Writes Martin Marty, "When nothing happens to protect injustice, the world makes known its disgust with the church. When something happens and the church is willing to risk unpopularity in its local community, the world watches. Even where the world does not share the courage —or even the idea—it is tantalized by the spirit and a force that after so many centuries burns anew in the lives of people who 'go about doing good'." [5] It is this same quality of translation that is one with Luther who translated the words of Scripture and discovered a spirit that insisted that a Christian is the true lord of all, slave of no one; therefore, the servant to everyone!

In Luther's day, the Christian community had to break out of the stylized forms which imprisoned it. In our time, there is another breaking out of accustomed forms and the urgency to communicate an idea. It is no longer respectable to hold a Christian faith in a compartmentalized life. The idea must be shared or deserted. This is the challenge, and it is similar to the test of the Reformation period. It is this principle which has motivated Lutheranism in its establishment of an ecumenical institute in Strasbourg, in the evangelical academies and mass movements of laymen in Germany, in the Faith and Life institutes in America, in the rethinking of theological education, in the furtherance of Biblical study, in the involvement of the church in the social issues of the day which range from nuclear energy to the problems of politics. It is this principle which ejects any parochial Lutheran into the struggle. It seems different than the academic business of translating a word from Latin into German but it is of the same discipline. It is the labor of the anonymous worker allowing the idea to escape.

The Christian Community · When the word "church" is mentioned, there is the image of both institution and fellowship. To the Lutheran it is the fellowship through which the expression of Word and Sacrament are shared. The *Augsburg Confession* declared that it "is sufficient for the true unity of the Christian church that the Gospel be preached in conformity with the pure understanding of it and that the sacraments be administered in accordance with the divine Word." In this faith the church is one. That's inherent in Lutheranism. It's not bound in hierarchies, organizations or traditions, not even in historic confessions of faith. The one, holy, apostolic church is a fact and it is in the recognition of that fact that the "church" becomes a life-filled, Spirit-guided fact.

There are harsh things said about the church as an institution but Lutherans have lived through this kind of history, understanding the need to renew the structure without destroying the form. The church knows episcopacies, democracies, federations and sometimes has seemed to exist despite chaos. Through this diversity of form there has been a uniting spirit. The same diversities typify the individual member. In faith he discovers his true individuality and his true community.

When the first Lutheran World Assembly gathered in Lund, Sweden, in 1946, only Lutherans were present. That was thrilling enough and satisfying. Yet this would have been lonesome and unrealistic in 1963 when the Fourth Assembly was held in Helsinki, Finland. Official visitors were present from all Protestant and Orthodox groups. Delegated observers were present from the Roman Catholic Church. What is more important, the observers were not just looking over the shoulders of the official delegates. In their own way they were a part of the total setting.

The church is known in the local parish, in the evangelical witness in councils in nation or world, or in the common search for the sense of a uniting Spirit. The history of the Lutheran communion is a history of self-criticism, of dynamic adventure and a willingness not to be limited by form. That is often obscured but the ferment is there for the bubbling fire of "one body and one Spirit, just as you were called to one hope that belongs to your call, one Lord, one faith, one baptism, one God and father of all who is above all and through all and in all." (Eph. 4:4–6) The same fellowship is subject to self-criticism. It does not have to be demolished to discover the essential dynamic of fellowship. This is the reformation that knows creative search for new expression of this reconciling love of God.

The Christian Family · At the heart of the expression of its faith, this fellowship of Lutherans has nurtured and strengthened the family. There its hymns and prayers were taught, its catechism learned and its way of life explained. Through the family, the lay leadership of the church found impetus as the whole family participated in the life and

program of the church. Difficult as it is to adapt these
ideals in the pressures of contemporary life, this is still the
structure and form of the Lutheran communion. To know
the Lutheran church is to know and to understand this
meaning of the Christian home and family. The devotional
life of the household is pressured by all of the influences
that are expressed in all of life. Yet this ideal is basic to
this way of life and is an important steeple in the struggle.

Ultimate Truth · When Jesus spoke of the kingdom of
God he told of a shepherd searching for a lost sheep; a
woman searching for a lost coin, or a father waiting for
his wayward son. There was an ultimate.

Death comes, life changes, yet there is hope of the
certainty of God's judgment and love. For the Lutheran,
there has not been the urgency of a purgatory or the
anxiety of a "second coming." There is the urgency of
the real presence which brings the quality of the ultimate
to the contemporary scene. A man's life has meaning in
the "now" because there is always a "now."

The late Paul Tillich wrote that this heritage, which
must be considered in the dialogue, is imperative. "The
Protestant principle took form in Luther's fight for justification by grace and through faith alone. 'Justification' in
this sense is the paradox that man, the sinner, is justified;
that man the unrighteous is righteous; that man the un-
holy is holy; namely, in the judgment of God, which is
not based on human achievements but only on divine,
self-surrendering grace." [6]

When the writers of the *Augsburg Confession* considered the statement of faith for the Lutheran community
they quoted St. Ambrose, "This is ordained of God, that
he that believeth in Christ shall be saved, without works,
by faith alone, freely receiving the remission of sins."
That was reason enough and in the sense of the ultimate

is the new vocation. The church can always face the insecurities of changing formations since she finds meaning in the Christ who is known beyond the formations and the formulations.

The Lutheran Church has had its times to speak; it must also listen. It is a part of the whole tradition of the generations. It knows its ancestors and its colleagues. Whatever differences there are—and there are many—between Roman Catholics and Lutherans or other Christian churches, there are more areas of agreement. They are the areas which demand consideration and conference. What is apparent now is that there is a great desire to carry on this dialogue, and that there might be, in our time, a serious restatement of the great evangelical tradition which believes that the living Word of God flows in and through the communion of saints. For Christ is the Lord of the Church.

What is it to be a Lutheran? It is to know this catholicity of experience and a reforming restlessness which is always in search of the Real Presence. It is to forget about being Lutheran. It is to know a dynamic, reforming spirit of the Living God through Word and Sacrament. It is to love Christ, believing that in the fellowship of believers there is the body of Christ in this world. Never equating contemporary program with the kingdom, never forsaking the immediate program to be lost in some vague otherworldliness gives vitality to ethics. It is to experience this grace of God in a world of nuclear energy, of vast unexplored spaces, of a world of cybernetics and new technocracy. It is not an attempt to perpetuate a sixteenth century church; it is a dynamic which believes that forgiveness is a continuing and creative force and searches for ways of sharing and expressing this witness in a true catholicity of experience. It is the freedom, and so the responsibility, to share in the continuing dialogue of faith.

In the world of the twentieth century there is a profound sense of anxiety. There is also an uncertainty about the continuance and meaning of human existence. Men talk in strange words of the fact that God is being crowded out of the world. It sounds strangely like the uncertainties which tortured Luther in the sixteenth century. To discover the continuing grace of God is to know the truth "and the truth will make you free." It is this assurance that God is known through Christ, sharing a freedom which enables a man of God to live in this world of new power without losing a sense of stability. The truth sets us free from the cynicism which becomes trapped in words and phrases, in secular forms and in contemporary hopelessness. These are but a few of the steeples in the struggle. There are others. They are the exclamation-points of trust, asserting:

> A mighty fortress is our God
> A bulwark never failing;
> Our helper he amid the flood
> Of mortal ills prevailing . . .
> That work above all earthly powers,
> No thanks to them, abideth;
> The spirit and the gifts are ours
> Through Him who with us sideth:
> Let good and kindred go,
> This mortal life also;
> The body they may kill:
> God's truth abideth still,
> His kingdom is forever.

Appendix

The Small Catechism

by *Martin Luther*

IN CONTEMPORARY ENGLISH

A *Handbook of Basic Christian
Instruction for the Family
and the Congregation*

Part One
THE TEN COMMANDMENTS

I am the Lord your God.

The First Commandment	*What does this mean for us?*
You shall have no other Gods.	We are to fear, love, and trust God above anything else.
The Second Commandment	*What does this mean for us?*
You shall not take the name of the Lord your God in vain.	We are to fear and love God so that we do not use his name to curse, swear, lie, or deceive, but call on him in prayer, praise, and thanksgiving.
The Third Commandment	*What does this mean for us?*
Remember the Sabbath day, to keep it holy.	We are to fear and love God so that we do not neglect his Word and the preaching of it, but regard it as holy and gladly hear and learn it.

The Fourth Commandment	*What does this mean for us?*
Honor your father and your mother.	We are to fear and love God so that we do not despise or anger our parents and others in authority, but respect, obey, love, and serve them.

The Fifth Commandment	*What does this mean for us?*
You shall not kill.	We are to fear and love God so that we do not hurt our neighbor in any way, but help him in all his physical needs.

The Sixth Commandment	*What does this mean for us?*
You shall not commit adultery.	We are to fear and love God so that in matters of sex our words and conduct are pure and honorable, and husband and wife love and respect each other.

The Seventh Commandment	*What does this mean for us?*
You shall not steal.	We are to fear and love God so that we do not take our neighbor's money or property, or get them in any dishonest way, but help him to improve and protect his property and means of making a living.

The Eighth Commandment	*What does this mean for us?*
You shall not bear false witness against your neighbor.	We are to fear and love God so that we do not betray, slander, or lie about our neighbor, but defend him, speak well of him, and explain his actions in the kindest way.

The Ninth Commandment	*What does this mean for us?*
You shall not covet your neighbor's house.	We are to fear and love God so that we de not desire to get our neighbor's possessions by scheming, or by pretending to have a right to them, but always help him keep what is his.

The Tenth Commandment	*What does this mean for us?*
You shall not covet your neighbor's wife, or his manservant, or his maid-servant, or his cattle, or anything that is your neighbor's.	We are to fear and love God so that we do not tempt or coax away from our neigbhor his wife or his workers, but encourage them to remain loyal.

What does God say of all these Commandments?	*What does this mean for us?*
He says: "I, the Lord your God, am a jealous God, visiting the iniquity of the fathers upon the children to the third and fourth genera-tion of those who hate me, but showing steadfast love to thousands of those who love me and keep my com-mandments."	God warns that he will punish all who break these command-ments. Therefore we are to fear his wrath and not disobey him. But he promises grace and every blessing to all who keep these commandments. Therefore we are to love and trust him, and gladly do what he commands.

Part Two
THE APOSTLES' CREED

The First Article	*What does this mean?*
I believe in God the Father almighty, Maker of heaven and earth.	I believe that God has created me and all that exists. He has given me and still

preserves my body and soul
with all their powers.

He provides me with food
and clothing, home and
family, daily work, and all
I need from day to day.
God also protects me in time
of danger and guards me from
every evil.

All this he does out of
fatherly and divine goodness
and mercy, though I do not
deserve it.
Therefore I surely ought to
thank and praise, serve and
obey him.

This is most certainly true.

What does this mean?

The Second Article

*And in Jesus Christ his only
Son, our Lord: who was
conceived by the Holy
Ghost, born of the Virgin
Mary: suffered under
Pontius Pilate, was cruci-
fied, dead, and buried; he
descended into hell; the
third day he rose again from
the dead; he ascended into
heaven, and sitteth on the
right hand of God the
Father almighty; from
thence he shall come to
judge the quick and the
dead.*

I believe that Jesus Christ—
true God, Son of the Father
from eternity, and true man,
born of the Virgin Mary—
is my Lord.

He has redeemed me, a lost
and condemned person, saved
me at great cost from sin,
death, and the power of the
devil—not with silver or gold,
but with his holy and precious
blood and his innocent
suffering and death.

All this he has done that I
may be his own, live under
him in his kingdom, and
serve him in everlasting
righteousness, innocence, and

blessedness, just as he is risen from the dead and lives and rules eternally.

This is most certainly true.

What does this mean?

The Third Article

I believe in the Holy Ghost: the holy Christian church, the communion of saints; the forgiveness of sins; the resurrection of the body; and the life everlasting. Amen.

I believe that I cannot by my own understanding or effort believe in Jesus Christ my Lord, or come to him.
But the Holy Spirit has called me through the gospel, enlightened me with his gifts, and sanctified and kept me in true faith.

In the same way he calls, gathers, enlightens, and sanctifies the whole Christian church on earth, and keeps it united with Jesus Christ in the one true faith.

In this Christian church day after day he fully forgives my sins and the sins of all believers.
On the last day he will raise me and all the dead and give me and all believers in Christ eternal life.

This is most certainly true.

Part Three
THE LORD'S PRAYER

The Introduction

Our Father who art in heaven.

What does this mean?

Here God encourages us to believe that he is truly our Father and we are his children.

We therefore are to pray to him with complete confidence just as children speak to their loving father.

The First Petition

Hallowed be thy name.

What does this mean?

God's name certainly is holy in itself, but we ask in this prayer that we may keep it holy.

When does this happen?

God's name is hallowed whenever his Word is rightly taught and we as children of God live in harmony with it. Help us to do this, heavenly Father!

But anyone who teaches or lives contrary to the Word of God dishonors God's name among us.
Keep us from doing this, heavenly Father!

The Second Petition

Thy kingdom come.

What does this mean?

God's kingdom comes indeed without our praying for it, but we ask in this prayer that it may come also to us.

When does this happen?

God's kingdom comes when our heavenly Father gives us his Holy Spirit, so that by his grace we believe his holy Word and live a godly life on earth now and in heaven forever.

The Third Petition

Thy will be done on earth as it is in heaven.

What does this mean?

The good and gracious will of God is surely done without our prayer, but we ask in this prayer that it may be done also among us.

When does this happen?

God's will is done when he hinders and defeats every evil scheme and purpose of the devil, the world, and our sinful self, which would prevent us from keeping his name holy and would oppose the coming of his kingdom. And his will is done when he strengthens our faith and keeps us firm in his Word as long as we live.

The Fourth Petition

Give us this day our daily bread.

What does this mean?

God gives daily bread, even without our prayer, to all people, though sinful, but we ask in this prayer that he will help us to realize this and to receive our daily bread with thanks.

What is meant by "daily bread"?

Daily bread includes everything needed for this life, such as food and clothing, home and property, work and income, a devoted family, an orderly community, good government, favorable weather, peace and health, a good name, and true friends and neighbors.

The Fifth Petition

And forgive us our trespasses, as we forgive those who trespass against us.

What does this mean?

We ask in this prayer that our Father in heaven would not hold our sins against us and because of them refuse to hear our prayer.

And we pray that he would give us everything by grace, for we sin every day and deserve nothing but punishment.

So we on our part will heartily forgive and gladly do good to those who sin against us.

The Sixth Petition

And lead us not into temptation.

What does this mean?

God tempts no one to sin, but we ask in this prayer that God would watch over us so that the devil, the world, and our sinful self may not deceive us and draw us into unbelief, despair, and other great and shameful sins.

And we pray that even though we are so tempted we may still win the final victory.

The Seventh Petition

But deliver us from evil.

What does this mean?

We ask in this inclusive prayer that our heavenly Father would save us from every evil to body and soul, and at our last hour would mercifully take

The Doxology

*For thine is the kingdom
and the power and the glory
forever and ever. Amen.*

us from the troubles of this
world to himself in heaven.

What does "Amen" mean?

Amen means *Yes, it shall
be so.*
We say Amen because we are
certain that such petitions are
pleasing to our Father in
heaven.
For he himself has commanded
us to pray in this way and
has promised to hear us.

Part Four
THE SACRAMENT OF BAPTISM

1
What is Baptism?
    The sacrament of Baptism is not water only,
    but it is water used together with God's Word
        and by his comand.
What is this Word?
    In Matthew 28 our Lord Jesus Christ says:
    "Go therefore and make disciples of all nations,
    baptizing them in the name of the Father and of
        the Son and of the Holy Spirit."

2
What benefits does God give in Baptism?
    In Baptism God forgives sin,
    delivers from death and the devil,
    and gives everlasting salvation to all who believe
        what he has promised.
What is God's promise?
    In Mark 16 our Lord Jesus Christ says:
    "He who believes and is baptized will be saved;
    but he who does not believe will be condemned."

3
How can water do such great things?
    It is not water that does these things,

but God's Word with the water and our trust in
    this Word.
Water by itself is only water,
but with this Word it is a life-giving water
which by grace gives the new birth through the
    Holy Spirit.
St. Paul writes in Titus 3:
"He saved us . . . in virtue of his own mercy,
by the washing of regeneration and renewal in
    the Holy Spirit,
which he poured out upon us richly
through Jesus Christ our Savior,
so that we might be justified by his grace
and become heirs in hope of eternal life.
The saying is sure."

4

What does Baptism mean for daily living?
    It means that our sinful self, with all its evil deeds
        and desires,
    should be drowned through daily repentance;
    and that day after day a new self should arise
    to live with God in righteousness and purity forever.
    St. Paul writes in Romans 6:
    "We were buried therefore with him by Baptism
        into death,
    so that as Christ was raised from the dead
        by the glory of the Father,
    we too might walk in newness of life."

Part Five
THE SACRAMENT OF HOLY COMMUNION

1

What is Holy Communion?
    It is the sacrament instituted by Christ himself,
    in which he gives us his body and blood
    in and with the bread and wine.

What are the Words of Institution?
  Our Lord Jesus Christ, in the night in which he
    was betrayed,
  took bread; and when he had given thanks,
  he broke it and gave it to his disciples,
  saying, "Take, eat, this is my body,
    which is given for you;
  this do in remembrance of me."
  After the same manner also he took the cup after
    supper,
  and when he had given thanks,
  he gave it to them, saying,
  "Drink of it, all of you;
  this cup is the new testament in my blood,
  which is shed for you, and for many, for the
    remission of sins;
  this do, as often as you drink it, in remembrance
    of me."

2

What benefits do we receive from this sacrament?
  The benefits of this sacrament are pointed out by
    the words,
  given and shed for you for the remission of sins.
  These words assure us that in the sacrament
  we receive forgiveness of sins, life, and salvation.
  For where there is forgiveness of sins,
  there is also life and salvation.

3

How can eating and drinking do all this?
  It is not eating and drinking that does this,
  but the words, *given and shed for you for the
    remission of sins.*
  These words, along with eating and drinking,
    are the main thing in the sacrament.
  And whoever believes these words
  has exactly what they say,
    forgiveness of sins.

4

When is a person rightly prepared to receive this sacrament?
Fasting and other outward preparation
  serve a good purpose.
However, that person is well prepared and
  worthy who believes these words,
given and shed for you for the remission of sins.
But anyone who does not believe these words, or
  doubts them,
is neither prepared nor worthy,
for the words *for you* require simply
  a believing heart.

THE OFFICE OF THE KEYS

What is the "Office of the Keys"?
It is that authority which Christ gave to his church to forgive the sins of those who repent and to declare to those who do not repent that their sins are not forgiven.

What are the words of Christ?
Our Lord Jesus Christ said to his disciples: "Receive the Holy Spirit. If you forgive the sins of any, they are forgiven; if you retain the sins of any, they are retained."—John 20:23

"Truly, I say to you, whatever you bind on earth shall be bound in heaven, and whatever you loose on earth shall be loosed in heaven."—Matthew 18:18

CONFESSION

What is private confession?
Private confession has two parts. First, we make a personal confession of sins to the pastor, and then we receive absolution, which means forgiveness as from God himself. This absolution we should not doubt, but firmly believe that thereby our sins are forgiven before God in heaven.

What sins should we confess?
Before God we should confess that we are guilty of all sins, even those which are not known to us, as we do in the Lord's Prayer. But in private confession, as before the

pastor, we should confess only those sins which trouble us in heart and mind.

What are such sins?

We can examine our everyday life according to the Ten Commandments—for example, how we act toward father or mother, son or daughter, husband or wife, or toward the people with whom we work, and so on. We may ask ourselves whether we have been disobedient or unfaithful, bad-tempered or dishonest, or whether we have hurt anyone by word or deed.

How might we confess our sins privately?

We may say that we wish to confess our sins and to receive absolution in God's name. We may begin by saying, "I, a poor sinner, confess before God that I am guilty of many sins." Then we should name the sins that trouble us. We may close the confession with the words, "I repent of all these sins and pray for mercy. I promise to do better with God's help."

What if we are not troubled by any special sins?

We should not torture ourselves with imaginary sins. If we cannot think of any sins to confess (which would hardly ever happen) we need not name any in particular, but may receive absolution because we have already made a general confession to God.

How may we be assured of forgiveness?

The pastor may pronounce the absolution by saying, "By the authority of our Lord Jesus Christ I forgive you your sins in the name of the Father and of the Son and of the Holy Spirit. Amen."

Those who are heavily burdened in conscience the pastor may comfort and encourage with further assurances from God's Word.

Notes and Bibliography

The volumes listed for each chapter are those which have been helpful personally and which will be of interest to those readers who desire to do further reading.

For Luther quotations, note:

L.W. refers to *The Works of Luther* (Philadelphia: A. J. Holman Co., 6 vols., 1915).

W.A. refers to *Martin Luther's Works* (Weimar Edition, 1883).

CHAPTER I: The Growing Edge

NOTES

1. Clifford E. Nelson, "Proceedings of the Fourth Assembly of the Lutheran World Federation," p. 291.

BIBLIOGRAPHY

Pelikan, Jaroslav, *The Riddle of Roman Catholicism*. Nashville: Abingdon Press, 1959.

Schmidt, John, *The Lutheran Confessions*. Philadelphia: Muhlenberg Press, 1956.

Kerr, Hugh Thomson, Jr., *A Compend of Luther's Theology*. Philadelphia: The Westminster Press, 1943.

Neve, I. L., *Introduction to Symbolical Books of the Lutheran Church*. Columbus, Ohio: Lutheran Book Concern, 1926.

Tavard, Georges, *Protestantism*. New York: Hawthorn Books Inc., 1959. Tavard is a perceptive Roman Catholic scholar who interprets the Reformation from his vantage point and poses interesting observations for the ecumenical situation.

CHAPTER II: At the Entrance

NOTES

1. Schmalkald Articles III, XII.

2. Heinrich Bornkamm, *Luther's World of Thought*, (St. Louis: Concordia, 1958).

3. Martin Luther, "Brief Explanation of Ten Commandments, Creed and Lord's Prayer." (L.W.), II, 368.

4. " 'Believing' is not a thing, but an event; it is primarily a verb and not as a noun that its reality is seen. Being affected (by the communication of faith) is not adequately expressed, or at least not without a possibility of misunderstanding, by the phrase, I have faith; nor by the expression, I am a believer; but simply by the words, I believe." Gerhard Ebeling, *The Nature of Faith* (Philadelphia: Muhlenberg Press), p. 109.

5. Martin Luther, "Epistle to Galatians," 2,340 (Erlangen Edition).

6. Martin Luther, "Essay on Translation," (L.W.).

7. It was a memorable moment when the Mass celebrated by Pope Paul VI at Yankee Stadium included the great chorale, beloved by Lutherans, "Nun Danket Alle Gott." Over the bridge of such hymnody we can join in a new search for Christian understanding.

8. Hans Lilje, *Luther Now* (Philadelphia: Muhlenberg Press, 1952), p. 144.

9. Dietrich Bonhoeffer, *The Cost of Discipleship* (New York: Macmillan Co., 1963), p. 47.

BIBLIOGRAPHY

Reed, Luther, *The Lutheran Liturgy*. Philadelphia: Muhlenberg Press, 1947.

Davis, H. Grady, *Why We Worship*. Philadelphia: Fortress Press, 1961.

CHAPTER III: The Christian Encounter

NOTES

1. Joseph Sittler, "Doctrine of the Word" (United Lutheran Publication, 1948), p. 5-6.

2. Bonhoeffer, *The Cost of Discipleship*, p. 103.

3. Heinrich Bornkamm, *The Heart of Reformation Faith* (New York: Harper & Row, 1948), p. 54.

4. Martin E. Marty (from an unpublished address given at an Ecumenical Forum in Buffalo in 1964).

5. Martin Heinecken, ed. Harold G. Letts, *Existence Today* (Philadelphia: Muhlenberg Press, 1957), p. 125.

6. Jonah Exegesis (1526).

BIBLIOGRAPHY

Baillie, Donald M., *God Was in Christ*. New York: Scribner's, 1948.

Nygren, Anders, *Commentary on Romans*. Philadelphia: Muhlenberg Press, 1949.

————, *The Gospel of God*. Philadelphia: The Westminster Press, 1951.

Fremantle, Anne, *Protestant Mystics*. Boston: Little, Brown and Co., 1964.

CHAPTER IV: The Freedom of the Christian

NOTES

1. Helmut Thielicke, *Nihilism* (New York: Harper & Brothers, 1961), p. 26.

2. Luther's Small Catechism. See Appendix.

3. Martin Luther, "A Treatise on Christian Liberty," (L.W.), II, 312.

4. Gerard Manley Hopkins, "God's Grandeur" *Poems of Gerard Manley Hopkins*, 3rd Edition (Oxford University Press, Inc., 1948).

5. See Proceedings of the Fourth Assembly of the Lutheran World Federation, Helsinki, Finland, Lutherisches Verlagshaus, Berlin, 1965.

6. Small Catechism, Explanation of Third Article, Apostles' Creed.

7. Martin Luther, "Magnificat."

8. Martin Luther, "Prefatory Remarks to Letter to the Romans" (1552).

9. Proceedings of the Fourth Assembly of the Luther World Federation, Helsinki, Finland, Lutherisches Verlagshaus, Berlin and Hamburg, 1963, p. 355.

BIBLIOGRAPHY
Justification Today. Publication of Lutheran World Federation, Geneva, Switzerland, 1963.
Whale, J. S., *The Protestant Tradition*. Cambridge, England, 1955.
Reu, M., *Catechetics*. Chicago: Wartburg Press, 1927.
Heinecken, Martin, *Basic Christian Teachings*. Philadelphia: Muhlenberg Press, 1959.
A *Reexamination of Lutheran and Reformed Traditions*, pamphlet pub. by National Lutheran Council, New York, 1965.

CHAPTER V: The Contemporary Voice

NOTES
1. Martin Luther, "Introduction to Old Testament-1545." (L.W.) VI, 368.
2. Martin Luther, (W.A.).
3. Martin Luther, (W.A.), 1,458.
4. Martin Luther, *Against Heavenly Prophets* (L.W.), 40:160.
5. Emil Brunner, *Revelation and Reason*. Trans., Olive Wyon (Philadelphia: The Westminster Press, Copyright 1946, W. L. Jenkins), p. 169.
6. Bonhoeffer, *Cost of Discipleship*.
7. Martin Luther, *Table Talk* (New York: World Publishing Company, 1952), p. 244.
8. Philip Schaff, *History of the Christian Church* (New York: Scribner's, 1918), II, 385ff.
9. Martin Luther (W.A.), 12:259ff.
10. Martin Luther (W.A.), 10 (Book I) 626.
11. K. E. Skydsgaard, *One in Christ* (Philadelphia: Muhlenberg Press, 1957), p. 162.
12. Grady Davis, "Nature, Love and Robert Frost" in *Scope of Grace*, ed. Philip Hefner (Philadelphia: Fortress Press, 1964).
13. Martin Luther (W.A.), 21, 22.

BIBLIOGRAPHY
Sittler, Joseph, *The Doctrine of the Word*. Philadelphia: Muhlenberg Press, 1948.

Watson, Philip S., *Let God Be God*. Philadelphia: Muhlenberg Press, 1948.

Pittenger, W. Norman, *The Word Incarnate*. New York: Harper & Brothers, 1959.

CHAPTER VI: The Hinges of Grace

NOTES

1. Martin Heinecken, *The Meaning and Practice of the Lord's Supper*, ed. H. T. Lehman (Philadelphia: Muhlenberg Press, 1961).

2. Helmut Thielicke, *The Silence of God* (Grand Rapids: Erdman Publishing Co., 1962), p. 18.

3. Gerhard Ebling, *Word and Faith* (Philadelphia: Fortress Press, 1963).

4. *Ibid.*

BIBLIOGRAPHY

Marty, Martin E., *Baptism*. Philadelphia: Muhlenberg Press, 1962.

Tappert, Theo. G., *The Lord's Supper*. Philadelphia: Muhlenberg Press, 1962.

Koenker, Ernest B., *Sacraments in Christian Worship*. St. Louis: Concordia, 1959.

———, *Worship in Word and Sacrament*. St. Louis: Concordia, 1959.

Allbeck, Willard D., *Studies in the Lutheran Confessions*. Philadelphia: Muhlenberg Press, 1952.

Lehman, Helmut T., *Meaning and Practise of the Lord's Supper*. Philadelphia: Muhlenberg Press, 1961.

Lindemann, Fred H., *Till He Come: A Study of the Lord's Supper*. New York: Ernest Kaufmann, Inc., 1948.

CHAPTER VII: The Priesthood of Believers

NOTES

1. Joseph C. McLelland, *Reformation and Significance Today* (Philadelphia: The Westminster Press, © 1962).

2. Luther in his Exposition of Psalm 147.

3. Roland Bainton, *The Reformation of the Sixteenth Century* (Boston: Beacon Press, 1953), p. 246.

4. Edgar M. Carlson, *Reinterpretation of Luther* (Philadelphia: Muhlenberg Press, 1948), p. 230.

5. Richard Luecke, *New Meanings for New Beings* (Philadelphia: Fortress Press, 1964), p. 235.

Note: One of the delightful, and typically plain-spoken comments of Martin Luther relevant to vocation occurs in his essay "Concerning Married Life," 1522:

"Along comes the clever harlot, namely natural reason, looks at married life, turns up her nose, and says, Why, must I rock the baby, wash its diapers, change its bed, smell its odour, heal its rash, take care of this and take care of that, do this and do that? It is better to remain single and live a quiet and carefree life. I will become a priest or a nun and tell my children to do the same.

"But what does the Christian faith say? The father opens his eyes, looks at these lowly, distasteful and despised things and knows that they are adorned with divine approval as with the most precious gold and silver. God, with his angels and creatures, will smile—not because diapers are washed, but because it is done in faith."

BIBLIOGRAPHY

Wingren, Gustaf, *Luther on Vocation*. Philadelphia: Muhlenberg Press, 1957.

Heuss, John, *Our Christian Vocation*. Greenwich, Connecticut: Seabury Press, 1955.

Luther, Martin, "Christian Liberty" in *The Three Treatises*. Philadelphia: Muhlenberg Press.

Loew, Ralph W., *The Church and the Amateur Adult*. Philadelphia: Muhlenberg Press, 1955.

"Spirituality In Church and World." New York: Paulist Press. A series of articles included in Volume 9 of *Concilium: Theology in the Age of Renewal*, an excellent statement of some of the exciting thinking articulate in Roman Catholic circles, encouraging new crossroads of meeting between Protestant and Roman Catholic laymen.

CHAPTER VIII: The Household of Faith
NOTES
1. Martin Luther (W.A.), VIII, 491.
2. E. Clifford Nelson, "Proceedings of the Fourth Assembly,

Lutheran World Federation, Helsinki, Finland, Lutherisches Verlagshaus, Berlin, 1963, p. 283.

3. K. E. Skydsgaard, *One in Christ* (Philadelphia: Muhlenberg Press, 1957), p. 183.

4. Mark Gibbs and T. Ralph Morton, *God's Frozen People* (Philadelphia: The Westminster Press, 1965), p. 174.

BIBLIOGRAPHY

Nygren, Anders, *This Is the Church*. Philadelphia: Muhlenberg Press, 1952.

Aulen, Gustaf, *Faith of the Christian Church*. Philadelphia: Muhlenberg Press, 1948.

Brown, Robert McAfee, *Spirit of Protestantism*. Oxford, 1961.

Bonhoeffer, Dietrich, *Life Together*. New York: Harper & Brothers, 1954.

Coates, Tomas, *Authority in the Church*. St. Louis: Concordia, 1964.

CHAPTER IX: The Heritage of Faith

NOTES

1. H. E. Jacobs, *Martin Luther* (New York: Putnam, 1902), p. 2.

2. Bonhoeffer, *The Cost of Discipleship*, pp. 52, 53.

3. Father Erwin Iserloh has stated that he does not believe that Luther affixed the Theses to the door of the Castle Church. Instead, he insists that Luther sent them to his Ordinary, the Auxiliary Bishop of Brandenburg and that he only published them after there was no answer. Moreover, says Father Iserloh, "It becomes even clearer that Luther did not boldly break with the Church, but that unintentionally he became a reformer." For a perceptive analysis of contemporary Catholic viewpoints of Luther, see "Do We Know the Others," edited by Hans Kung, vol. 14 of *Concilium* (New York: Paulist Press, 1966). The Iserloh article is one of the chapters of this volume.

4. Will Durant, *The Reformation* (New York: Simon and Schuster, 1957), p. 357.

5. Paul Tillich, *The Protestant Era* (Chicago: University of Chicago Press, 1948), p. 174.

6. Pelikan, *The Riddle of Roman Catholicism*, p. 50.

7. Jaroslav Pelikan, *Obedient Rebels* (New York: Harper & Row, 1964), p. 104.

8. Josephus F. M. S. Lescraawaet, "The Reformed Churches." An Essay in Fundamental Theology. *The Church and the World*, Johannes B. Metz, Editorial Director, VI of *Concilium*, (New York: Paulist Press, 1965), pp. 138–139.

BIBLIOGRAPHY

Marty, Martin E., *A Short History of Christianity*. New York: Meridian, 1959.

Böhmer, Heinrich, *Luther in Light of Recent Research*. Philadelphia: Christian Herald, 1916.

———, *Road to Reformation*. Philadelphia: Muhlenberg Press, 1946.

Schweibert, E. G., *Luther and His Times*. St. Louis, Concordia, 1950.

Bainton, Roland, *Here I Stand*. Nashville: Abingdon Press, 1950.

Erikson, Erik H., *Young Man Luther*. New York: W. W. Norton & Company, 1958.

Ritter, Gerhard, *Luther*. New York: Harper & Row, 1959.

Hillebrand, Hans J., *The Reformation*. New York: Harper & Row, 1964.

CHAPTER X: The American Translation

NOTES

1. Paul Gerhardt, Hymn 579, *Service Book and Hymnal* (Lutheran Church in America), 1958.

2. Dr. Richard C. Wolf typifies the ministry of Muhlenberg as "a legacy of no mean proportions—a church which was both demonstrably Lutheran and demonstrably American." Richard C. Wolf, *Lutherans in North America* (Lutheran Church Press, 1965), p. 33.

3. Albert Standerman, *Our New Church*, (Philadelphia: Fortress Press, 1962).

4. *Minutes* (Lutheran Church in America, 1964), p. 12.

BIBLIOGRAPHY

Stauderman, Albert, *Our New Church*. Philadelphia: Lutheran Church Press, 1962.

Wentz, Frederick W., *Lutherans and Other Denominations*. Philadelphia: Lutheran Church Press, 1964.

Weiser, Frederick, *Love's Response*. Board of Publication, United Lutheran Church in America, 1962.

Wentz, Abdel R., *Basic History of Lutheranism in America*. Philadelphia: Muhlenberg Press, 1955.

Brauer, Jerald, *Protestantism in America*. Philadelphia: The Westminster Press, 1966.

Lund-Quist, Carl, *Lutheran Churches of the World*. Minneapolis: Augsburg Publishing Co., 1957.

CHAPTER XI: The Whole Man

NOTES

1. Dietrich Bonhoeffer, *Ethics* (New York: Macmillan, 1955), p. 264.

2. *Service Book and Hymnal* of the Lutheran Church in America, 1958, p. 287.

3. Luther Reed, *The Lutheran Liturgy* (Philadelphia: Muhlenberg Press, 1947), p. 4.

4. Luecke, *New Meanings for New Beings*, pp. 112–113.

5. Edward S. Frey, *This Before Architecture* (Jenkintown, Pa.: Foundation Books, 1963), p. 88.

6. Edgar S. Brown, Jr., "The Worship of the Church and Modern Man" in *New Theology No. 1*, ed. Martin E. Marty and Dean G. Peerman, (New York: Macmillan Co., 1965).

7. Martin Luther (W.A.), 596.

8. Daniel Callahan, *Honesty in the Church* (New York: Scribner's, 1965), p. 188.

BIBLIOGRAPHY

Tillich, Paul, *Theology of Culture*. Oxford University Press, 1959.

Niebuhr, Richard, *Christ and Culture*. New York: Harper & Brothers, 1951.

Robinson, John A. T., *Liturgy Coming to Life*. Philadelphia: The Westminster Press, 1960.

Hazelton, Roger, *New Accents in Contemporary Theology*. New York: Harper & Row, 1960.

Forell, George, Harold Grimm, Theo. Hoelty-Nickel, *Luther and Culture*. Luther College Press, 1960.

CHAPTER XII: The World of the Christian

NOTES

1. Martin Luther (W.A.), 101 38 (Advent, 1522 Matt. 21: 1–9) Weimar Edition.

2. Augsburg Confession, Article XVI.

3. A carefully worded statement indicating the precise re-statements of the Lutheran position of Church and State was adopted by a recent convention of the Lutheran Church in America. It emphasizes the "institutional separation and functional interaction" of church and state. "By institutional separation we mean that church and state must each be free to perform its essential task under God." The statement recognizes the need to restudy relationships in a pluralistic society insisting that the church must encourage citizenship, championing human rights. On the other hand the state must guarantee religious liberty, acknowledging that the rights of man are not the creation of the state, and providing assistance for educational and social benefits which church agencies render for the secular benefit of the community.
The full statement is listed in the Reports to the Convention of the Lutheran Church in America (1966), p. 366.

4. Joseph Sittler, *Structure of Christian Ethics* (Baton Rouge, La.: Louisiana State University, 1958), p. 13.

5. George Forell, *Faith Active in Love* (New York: American Press, 1954), p. 111.

6. William H. Lazareth, "The Theology of Politics," Statement of Board of Social Ministry, Lutheran Church in America, pp. 23–24.

BIBLIOGRAPHY

Berger, Peter L., *The Precarious Vision*. New York: Doubleday, 1964.

Aulen, Gustaf, *Church Law and Society*. New York: Scribner's, 1948.

Simon, Arthur, *Faces of Poverty*. St. Louis: Concordia, 1966.

Nygren, Anders, *Agape and Eros.* 3 vols., New York: Macmillan Co.

Brunner, Emil, *Justice and the Social Order.* New York: Harper & Row, 1945.

Letts, Harold C., ed., *Christian Social Responsibility*, 3 vols. Philadelphia: Muhlenberg Press, 1957.

Thielicke, Helmut, *Nihilism.* New York: Harper & Row, 1961.

Scherer, Paul E., *The Plight of Freedom.* New York: Harper & Row, 1948.

CHAPTER XIII: Steeples in the Struggle

NOTES

1. Dietrich Bonhoeffer, *No Rusty Sword* (New York: Harper & Row, 1965), p. 344.

2. Martin E. Marty, *Second Chance for American Protestants* (New York: Harper & Row, 1964), p. 164.

3. Paul E. Scherer, *The Word God Sent* (New York: Harper & Row, 1966), p. 29.

4. Richard Niebuhr, *Christ and Culture* (New York: Harper & Row, 1951).

5. Martin E. Marty, *The Improper Opinion* (Philadelphia: The Westminster Press, 1961), p. 117.

6. Tillich, *The Protestant Era,*

BIBLIOGRAPHY

Boyer, Merle William, *Luther in Protestantism Today.* New York: Association Press, 1958.

Hong, Howard, *This World and the Church.* Minneapolis: Augsburg Publishing Co., 1955.

Nash, Arnold, ed., *Protestant Thought in the Twentieth Century.* New York: Macmillan Co., 1951.

Michalson, Carl, *The Hinge of History.* New York: Scribner's, 1959.

In addition, there are numerous articles appearing in a variety of publications, especially in:

"Dialog," A quarterly. Minneapolis: Dialog, Inc.

"Lutheran World," A publication of the Lutheran World Federation, published by Lutheran World Federation, Geneva, Switzerland, especially "Faith and Society," an article published May, 1966.

Index